Critical Reading

Experienced scientists and medical researchers know how important it is to engage with research literature in an active, critical and analytical way. However, in most universities little time is devoted to teaching the relevant skills. Readers who accept scientific papers uncritically may misunderstand results, misinterpret methods, over- or under-estimate the importance of findings and waste time and resources on flawed or unnecessary experiments.

Critical Reading is aimed at everyone who needs to read original research papers in life sciences and medicine: final-year undergraduates, graduate students, research scientists, clinicians and medical researchers. Through a series of clearly focused chapters, the reader is introduced to critical reading skills such as

- detection and analysis of spin
- development of active reading habits
- evaluation of methods, including quantitative methods
- scientific analysis and interpretation

This book promotes a balanced, rigorous approach to the literature. It is unique in providing examples and end-of-chapter exercises from a wide range of scientific and clinical disciplines including biochemistry, ecology, immunology, molecular biology and physiology. Principles are extensively illustrated by reference to real papers, which are discussed constructively in the context of the pressures and technical difficulties that face researchers.

The skills *Critical Reading* imparts will deepen readers' understanding of the research process, increase enjoyment and enhance professional confidence and effectiveness in academic, clinical and commercial settings.

Ben Yudkin teaches at the Department for Continuing Education, University of Oxford, UK, where he runs graduate courses in critical literature interpretation and experimental techniques in molecular biology.

Critical Reading

*Making sense of research papers
in life sciences and medicine*

Ben Yudkin

Routledge
Taylor & Francis Group

LONDON AND NEW YORK

First published 2006 by Routledge
2 Park Square, Milton Park, Abingdon, Oxon OX14 4RN

Simultaneously published in the USA and Canada
by Routledge
270 Madison Ave, New York, NY 10016

Routledge is an imprint of the Taylor & Francis Group

© 2006 Ben Yudkin

Typeset in Goudy by RefineCatch Ltd, Bungay, Suffolk
Printed and bound in Great Britain by
TJ International, Padstow, Cornwall

British Library Cataloguing in Publication Data
A catalogue record for this book is available from the British Library

Library of Congress Cataloging in Publication Data
Yudkin, Ben, 1968–
Critical reading : making sense of papers in life sciences and
medicine / Ben Yudkin.
p. cm.
Includes bibliographical references and index.
1. Medical literature – Evaluation.   2. Life sciences
literature – Evalution.   3. Critical thinking.   4. Content area reading.
I. Title.
R118.6.Y85 2006
610–dc22   2005020922

ISBN10: 0–415–34413–1 (hbk)
ISBN10: 0–415–30322–2 (pbk)

ISBN13: 978–0–415–34413–5 (hbk)
ISBN13: 978–0–415–30322–4 (pbk)

Contents

Contents

Figures

Preface

When I describe this book to colleagues, they light up and tell me what a brilliant idea it is. When I go on to explain that all the examples and exercises are taken from real papers, they tend to look at me askance and – often quite loudly – question the sanity of anybody who would spend a whole book demolishing other people's work. Let me address both these reactions.

The idea for this book came from Dilys Alam, my commissioning editor at Taylor & Francis. Dilys articulated what university teachers have known for years: that every scientist needs to read original research papers, but few, historically, have been taught how to do it. This has left critical literature interpretation in a peculiar position. Empirical research forms the entire basis of modern medicine and science. There is arguably no more universally important activity for life scientists and medics across the board than understanding and evaluating the published research of their colleagues. Yet the assumption has been that the necessary skills of critical scrutiny and careful analysis will somehow develop by themselves.

Until recently, that is. The past few years have seen a proliferation of university courses on reading, analysis and evaluation of literature in life sciences, medicine and biomedical sciences. Students in the United States, the UK, Australia and elsewhere can now gain credits in 'Analysis of Biological Literature', 'Evaluating Health Research Literature', 'Critical Evaluation of Literature' and so on. It is hoped that this book will provide a timely and helpful text to accompany many of those courses.

What about the use of real papers to illustrate good – and not so good – practice? The tens of examples used within the text and in the end-of-chapter exercises are drawn from a wide range of fields in biological and clinical sciences. Isn't this kind of criticism a sure way to make enemies? I do not believe it is, for two reasons. First, once a piece of research has been put in the public domain, it is open to critical evaluation by others. Scientists recognise that their work can advance only when it takes place in an atmosphere of free enquiry and discussion. When they publish, they expect a reaction, even if that reaction does not support their interpretation unreservedly. Second, this book is not about highlighting the negative. It is about approaching literature with an open mind and above all recognising that the process of scientific investigation is a genuine challenge subject to the same pressures and constraints as any other human activity. Many of the examples have in fact been selected for entirely positive reasons; in the others, I have tried to analyse possible limitations rather than merely indicating instances of failure. The discussions of real papers take this balanced perspective as their starting point. If I have fallen short in that balance by misrepresenting anyone's work, then the fault is entirely mine: that has certainly not been the intention.

HOW TO USE THIS BOOK

The book is designed to be clear and accessible. Chapters are divided into short sections and subsections, and each chapter ends with a brief summary. Key points are highlighted thus:

☞   **This is an important point**

A central part of each chapter is its 'Papers in Focus', where principles of critical reading are illustrated using extracts from real papers. Many of the chapters end with exercises in which readers are asked to comment on excerpts also taken from real papers. It should be stressed that the extracts are just that – short citations taken from whole papers. For the purposes of the exercise, you are asked to comment on the extract in isolation, but it is worth bearing in mind that in real life, the rest of the paper may answer some of the questions or criticisms that you have about the isolated passage. The examples have been chosen to cover as wide as possible a range of disciplines. It is hoped that readers with diverse backgrounds will find examples to suit them within the exercises. I do not imagine that any but the most adventurous will wish to tackle every single piece selected.

I hope that this book will provide a stimulating foray into the literature for academic, industrial and clinical scientists, and that its readers will share my enjoyment in discovering such a wealth of interesting and ingenious science.

Oxford, August 2005

Acknowledgements

Any book is a collaborative effort, and this one has been particularly so as I have sought to familiarise myself with a large body of literature in diverse fields. David Harris, Louis Mahadevan, Jane Mellor, Arnold Monto and Michael Thun in particular have taken the trouble to help me understand individual subject areas or papers. I am grateful to them, and to the many other people who suggested illustrative examples from the research literature. I thank Michael Yudkin, who spent a great deal of time illuminating difficult papers and suggesting fruitful avenues of enquiry. His constant readiness with time and ideas has been a great source of encouragement and stimulation. I am indebted to Pat Yudkin for extensive discussions about the numerical and statistical aspects of the text at all stages of writing. Her invaluable comments and wealth of experience have helped to shape Chapter 6 in particular.

Patti Quant provided many helpful suggestions and numerous contacts at the very beginning of this project. The authors whom I approached about using their work in exercises were almost universally supportive, and many critical reading teachers with whom I have corresponded have expressed great interest in the book as well as providing practical help. All have my thanks for their generosity and enthusiasm.

My commissioning editor, Dilys Alam, was instrumental in supporting the early stages of this project, when the manuscript was first being coaxed from an embryonic idea. Her successor, Philip Mudd, has provided many helpful insights and comments during later phases. I am grateful to both of them, and their respective editorial teams, for their hard work, professionalism and good humour throughout. Thanks too to production manager Colin Morgan and copy-editor Jane Olorenshaw for their efficiency and care.

For her unflagging support, encouragement and love, as well as for innumerable critical improvements to the manuscript, I thank my wife Carol from the bottom of my heart.

1

The paper trail

THE DEEP END

When you study from a textbook, quite a lot of the book is devoted to explaining the background to each topic and any technical terms. Pick up a research paper, however, and it is likely that the first words you read will be jargon, relying on previous knowledge. Even the title can be intimidating. The experience is not unlike watching your first episode of a long-running soap opera. Who is Ryan's real father? Why does Tina hate Ashley so much? And what does the Seafront Diner have to do with Slammer's prison sentence?

The fact is that space in journals is limited and authors of research papers, as well as journal editors, are concerned to cut out as much material as possible. Papers are aimed at specialist readers and not generally at people coming to the subject for the first time. Authors expect their readers to be familiar with the field, and do not take up much space explaining the background to their experiments. A description of the background science, an account of which areas are currently attracting research attention and an explanation of the terminology all take up space, and they are generally dealt with only briefly.

This is all very well if you are an expert; however, if you have not been working in the field for long and do not know the latest developments, it can be offputting. This chapter is about how to locate the background knowledge you need in order to tackle original research papers.

Paper in focus

Nurse, P. (1975) 'Genetic control of cell size at cell division in yeast', *Nature* 256: 547–51.

Cell division is a tightly regulated process. Cells must not divide until they have grown large enough. They must not divide unless all the DNA has been replicated. On the other hand, cell division must go ahead eventually if the organism is to grow. Understanding the genetic regulation of normal cell division is of particular interest because cancer involves a breakdown in this regulation. Yeasts have proved a fruitful model organism for studying cell division: they are simple eukaryotes that are easy to culture and study, yet the mechanisms for controlling cell division are remarkably similar to those in higher organisms, so that studying yeasts can tell us about people too.

The Abstract reads as follows:

A temperature-sensitive mutant strain of the fission yeast *Schizosaccharomyces pombe* has been isolated which divides at half the size of the wild type. Study of this strain suggests that there is a cell size control over DNA synthesis and a second control acting on nuclear division.

☞ The Abstract contains a brief summary of the results

Quite a lot of background knowledge has been assumed. What is fission yeast? What is a temperature-sensitive mutant? And, perhaps most fundamentally, why is this a useful experiment?

For those working in the field, it may be obvious which topics are calling out to be studied, but the rest of us may need some clues. Every field has its 'hot topics' – areas that are of particular interest at the moment. The Abstract summarises the results, but sometimes omits a description of why the experiment was performed. The Introduction should supply this, at least briefly, and it is important to read the Introduction before going any further. The Introduction to this paper begins:

Growing cells tend to maintain a constant size at division[1-3]. This implies that there is coordination between cellular growth and cell division which results in a division occurring when the cell has grown to a particular size. The mechanism by which this is achieved remains obscure although there are various theoretical models which could account for the phenomenon[4]. A new approach to the problem would be the study of mutant strains in which the normal coordination between cellular growth and cell division is disrupted, resulting in the division of cells at different sizes.

Here, the author gives a rationale for his 1975 experiment. The assumption is that there are genes that control the size that a cell has to reach before it divides, and the idea of the experiment is to understand how the normal genes work by studying what happens when they go wrong. It is a powerful and widely used genetic technique. Nurse went on to win the Nobel Prize for his discoveries.

☞ **The Introduction should tell you why the experiment was performed**

We shall discuss the Abstract and the Introduction in more detail in Chapter 4. But what about the questions raised by the Abstract, questions about the techniques and technical terms used? The Introduction will not answer these. A familiarity with the scientific background is assumed.

SOURCES OF INFORMATION

Textbooks

Textbooks are ideal for answering the more basic kinds of query. A cell biology or genetics textbook will probably have 'yeast' or '*Schizosaccharomyces*' in the index. If your interest is mainly in the way cell division is regulated, you will not need much detail on the biology of yeasts, but you will need to have some idea of yeast genetics and perhaps to know a bit about how yeasts are cultured. Similarly, a genetics textbook will have 'temperature-sensitive mutation' in the index (under either 'temperature-sensitive' or 'mutation').

Do not get too bogged down with textbooks. Ploughing through every word can confuse the issue with unnecessary detail that makes the basic arguments and their relationships harder to remember. Fortunately, most modern textbooks are well designed in short sections with clear sub-headings. It is worth skimming the sub-headings in the chapter of interest for two reasons. First, skimming points us to the most relevant parts of a chapter. Second, skimming allows readers to wander from the page where they have been directed by the index, and to check whether something important is hiding in a nearby chapter section. Some textbooks have detailed tables of contents at the front that list all the sub-headings. Reading the detailed contents is often an excellent way to obtain a brief summary of the chapter. Once you have homed in on a relatively small number of pages, reading them in detail is not so laborious.

☞ **Textbook headings can be skimmed to home in on what you want**

Reviews

Sometimes the background knowledge assumed in a research paper is specialised. There may be some aspects that particularly interest us or that we need to know in more detail than a textbook can provide. The following example is from a research paper about plant cell wall growth. As we shall see, some of the background is probably too specific to find in a general textbook, whereas it can be found in review papers.

Paper in focus

Reiter, W.-D., Chapple, C.C.S. and Somerville, C.R. (1993) 'Altered growth and cell walls in a fucose-deficient mutant of *Arabidopsis*', *Science* 261: 1032–5.

This paper appears on the second-year biology reading list of a well-known university. From the title it appears quite specialised, and the Abstract is also rather technical. However, the end of the Abstract suggests that, whatever the biochemical and genetic details of the mutant described in the paper, its biological effect is profound:

The mutant plants were dwarfed in growth habit, and their cell walls were considerably more fragile than normal.

Even without following the technical details in the Abstract, the reader is given some idea of what the paper will be about. As usual, the Introduction describes in brief why this research was performed:

The primary cell wall of higher plants determines cell shape and size during plant growth and development. Cell walls also provide mechanical support for plant tissues and organs and are intimately involved in a multitude of biological processes, such as cell-cell recognition and interaction, defense responses, and tropic responses (1). Plant cell walls are primarily composed of the polysaccharide components cellulose, hemicelluloses, and pectins (2). Cellulose microfibrils cross-linked by xyloglucan molecules are believed to serve as major load-bearing elements within the wall; however, the precise functions of the noncellulose cell wall polyscaccharides are poorly understood. To elucidate the roles of individual cell wall polysaccharides and to clone genes involved in their synthesis, we have taken a genetic approach by screening mutagenised *Arabidopsis* plants for alterations in their polysaccharide composition.

The authors have clearly explained why plant cell walls are important, and have enumerated some of their component polysaccharides. They have explained that the details of each polysaccharide's function are unclear. In order to find out more, they have used an approach similar to the one in the first example: by making artificial mutants and studying what happens when the polysaccharides are disrupted, the researchers have discovered something about how they function in the normal plant.

For this paper, you could look up '*Arabidopsis*' or 'polysaccharide' in a textbook. However, a general text would be unlikely to give details about how exactly cell walls are involved in cell-cell recognition, defence and tropism. More particularly, a textbook will probably say very little about how these functions of cell walls were discovered. To find this out, it may be helpful to read a review of the subject.

Review papers give an overview of an area of research by summarising research papers in the field. Typically, many tens or some hundreds of papers are reviewed. This saves you the work of finding and reading all the original research, and gives a summary of any trends in the results.

☞ **Review papers summarise and explain recent research in a field**

The Introduction quoted above refers to further papers. For example, reference 1 directs us to papers illustrating the roles of cell walls in biological processes. The reference reads as follows:

1. J.E. Varner and L.-S. Lin, *Cell* **56**, 231 (1989); K. Roberts, *Curr. Opin. Cell Biol.* **2**, 920 (1990); S. Levy and L.A. Staehelin, *ibid.* **4**, 856 (1992); N.C. Carpita and D.M. Gibeaut, *Plant J.* **3**, 1 (1993).

Note that a single reference includes several papers; this is a space-saving device used in the journal *Science*, from which this example is taken. Rather annoyingly, also to save space, neither the titles nor the finishing page-numbers of the papers are given. This makes it impossible to guess which papers are likely to be useful or how long they are without looking them up. Finally, the journal names are generally abbreviated; this will be discussed in the next section.

If you look up these four papers, you will find that they are all reviews. The full references are:

Varner, J.E. and Lin, L.-S. (1989) 'Plant cell wall architecture', *Cell* 56: 231–9.
Roberts, K. (1990) 'Structures at the plant cell surface', *Curr. Opin. Cell Biol.* 2: 920–8.
Levy, S. and Staehelin, L.A. (1992) 'Synthesis, assembly and function of plant cell wall macromolecules', *Curr. Opin. Cell Biol.* 4: 856–62.
Carpita, N.C. and Gibeaut, D.M. (1993) 'Structural models of primary cell walls in flowering plants: consistency of molecular structure with the physical properties of the walls during growth', *Plant J.* 3: 1–30.

The *Cell* paper is headed 'Review' and the *Plant Journal* paper is headed 'Major review'. The other two papers come from a journal whose title begins *Current Opinion in . . .*, which suggests a journal dedicated to review articles.

Knowing how to skim reviews for the most relevant parts is a useful skill, just as it is with textbooks. Different parts of a review will be useful for different people. A graduate student about to embark on a Ph.D. in plant cell wall biochemistry may well decide to read all these reviews in their entirety. On the other hand, an undergraduate writing an essay on plant cell walls may wish to read only small parts of reviews. For example, the review by Roberts contains a sub-heading 'Cell walls with altered compositions should help our understanding of architecture and function'; this seems a promising place to start if you simply want a bit of background to the research by Reiter *et al*.

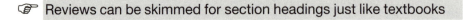
☞ Reviews can be skimmed for section headings just like textbooks

Research papers

While textbooks and reviews will sometimes give you all the background information you need, it will often be necessary to read other original research papers. This can seem daunting: if I need to read two more research papers in order to understand the one I am really interested in, maybe I will need to read a further four to understand those two, and so on. There is some justification for that fear. As against this, remember that when you read a paper together with relevant references, you are not simply laying down a linear trail of facts. The whole technique of reading and researching ensures that you finish with a broad and integrated view of the subject, a fully fledged concept map: in other words, you become a minor expert. Thinking, consolidation and revision are all rolled into one.

Paper in focus

Arioli, T., Peng, L., Betzner, A.S., Burn, J., Wittke, W., Herth, W., Camilleri, C., Höfte, H., Plazinski, J., Birch, R., Cork, A., Glover, J., Redmond, J. and Williamson, R.E. (1998) 'Molecular analysis of cellulose biosynthesis in *Arabidopsis*', *Science* 279: 717–20.

Here is another paper about structural polysaccharides in plants, but with a particular twist. Let us launch straight into the Abstract.

Cellulose, an abundant, crystalline polysaccharide, is central to plant morphogenesis and to many industries. Chemical and ultrastructural analyses together with map-based cloning indicate that the *RSW1* locus of *Arabidopsis* encodes the catalytic subunit of cellulose synthase. The cloned gene complements the *rsw1* mutant whose temperature-sensitive allele is changed in one amino acid. The mutant allele causes a specific reduction in cellulose synthesis . . .

The Introduction makes it clear how important cellulose is, and explains that the mechanism of cellulose synthesis by plants is poorly understood and that the genes responsible have not been cloned.

Cellulose, a crystalline β-1,4-glucan, is the world's most abundant biopolymer. Its biomass makes it a global carbon sink and renewable energy source, and its crystallinity provides mechanical properties central to plant morphogenesis and the fiber industries. The mechanisms that plants use in synthesis have not yielded to biochemistry or cloning by hybridization to genes encoding prokaryotic cellulose synthases (1). By combining chemical and ultrastructural analyses with map-based cloning, we show that the *Arabidopsis RSW1* locus encodes a glycosyl transferase that complements the *rsw1* mutant (2).

Textbooks and reviews will offer the usual help. For this paper, for instance, the concept of genetic complementation seems central to the experimental results.

Even with that information, something crucial would be missing. This whole paper is based on studying one particular mutant, and the experimental technique seems to depend on recognising plants that are mutant and those that are normal. Yet it is unlikely that a botany text would refer to *RSW1* in the index: the name and details of this particular gene are specialised knowledge, important for understanding our paper, but not an essential piece of general background for the average botany student.

A review might help, but the details of an individual gene and previous work on it would probably not be covered at length unless the gene is of central importance to the field. Instead, the review would probably refer you to the research paper in which the gene was first described.

In fact, you do not need to read a review to find that paper: it is referred to directly in the text. Thus, reference 2 of our paper is

2. T.I. Baskin, A.S. Betzner, R. Hoggart, A. Cork, R.E. Williamson, *Aust. J. Plant Physiol.* **19**, 427 (1992).

This turns out to be a paper called 'Root morphology mutants in *Arabidopsis thaliana*'. The paper describes mutations causing radial swelling of the root apex, which the authors name *rsw* mutants. There are photographs that show exactly what the mutants look like, and a discussion of what might be wrong biochemically with the plants having the Rsw appearance. In particular, the authors suggest, 'It is possible that the alignments of either the cortical microtubules or the cellulose are abnormal in one or all of these mutants.' A detailed reading of the paper is not necessary: we have what we need in order to understand our paper and its importance.

☞ **Original research papers are the place to find specific experimental details**

Looking up the reference has also given us an interesting insight into the scientific research process. Note that the Paper in Focus and this reference have some authors in common. Specifically, the last author is the same in both papers. By convention, the head of a research group is listed as the last author or 'senior author' on all the group's papers, and so both of these papers come from Williamson's group. The earlier paper was published in a specialist plant journal, while the second was published in the general and very widely read international journal *Science*. We can speculate that, having found mutant plants with an interesting and possibly cellulose-related abnormality, the group went on to study the mutants in more detail and eventually cloned a gene of general interest and importance.

FINDING WHAT YOU NEED

It is all very well knowing where to obtain information in principle, but actually finding the most helpful book, review or research paper among the huge number available can be like looking for a needle in a haystack. Fortunately, the haystack in this case is catalogued; nevertheless, the relevant databases are so large that efficient search strategies are needed.

Know your books

The title of a book may not be the same as the name of the subject you are looking for. In one of the examples above, we wanted to find out more about complementation. Looking for a book called 'Genetic Complementation' in the library would clearly not be a sensible way to find this information. It would be more fruitful to look for a general genetics textbook.

For general queries of this kind, it is helpful to cultivate a small number of favourite general texts that you find clear and easy to use. People differ in which books they prefer, but once you have found one or two that you like in each broad area, they will be able to help you with the majority of general questions. Lecturers, tutors, students and researchers who have studied the topic before are all good sources of book recommendations.

☞ Colleagues and tutors can recommend textbooks

Know your journals

The references cited so far have one thing in common: the journal name is always abbreviated. This is not a problem if you are familiar with the journals cited, but can be if you are trying to locate a reference in a journal you have not come across before.

Librarians are highly skilled at dealing with exactly this kind of query, and you should never be nervous about asking. Your librarian may well know not only the full name of the journal you are looking for, but also what its shelfmark is, where to find it and what colour binding you should be looking for. On one recent occasion, a book I was reading referred to a journal not listed in the library catalogue, and I asked the librarian for advice. Within minutes, he brought me the exact article I was looking for, having somehow discovered that the journal was in fact on the library shelves but that the journal name, the year of publication and the name of the paper's author were all misprinted in the book!

☞ A good librarian is a mine of useful infomation

There are also bibliographical resources that can help. A book called *Periodical Title Abbreviations* (Alkire 2004) tells you the title of a journal if you know the abbreviation, or *vice versa*. Hence, if you have a reference to *FEBS Lett.*, the book will tell you that the journal's full name is *The Federation of European Biochemical Societies Letters*; you may need the full name to search a catalogue, and it will help to give some idea what the journal is likely to be about. There are also online resources that can help with similar enquiries; for example, BioABACUS at <http://darwin.nmsu.edu/~molbio/bioABACUShome.htm> lets you search for all sorts of acronyms and abbreviations in biotechnology, including journal names.

The name of a journal often says something about what type of content to expect, as well as the subject area. In particular, some journals are devoted to review articles; these tend to have names beginning with phrases like *Current Opinion in . . ., Trends in . . .* or *Annual Review of. . ..* If you have several references to choose from and are looking specifically for a review, choosing one of these journals can help, though by doing so you will miss reviews in other journals that publish both reviews and original research papers.

Hunting the needle

Imagine that you are about to start a project on the effects of commercial sea fishing on marine mammal populations and wish to find some textbooks on the subject. How do you decide what to search for in a library catalogue? The quickest way is to make an educated guess and refine it by trial and error. The process can be very quick now that many library catalogues are available in searchable electronic form. Here are the results of my search:

```
1. Subject: fishing                      2695 records
```

The first few of these books were about angling. This was clearly not a useful place to start, and was a good illustration of why this process is called 'trial and error'.

   2. Subject: marine mammals   58 records

This list was short enough to look through the book titles quickly, and one of the entries turned out to be a book called *Whales, Seals, Fish and Man* (Blix *et al.* 1995). This looked promising, so I viewed the full library record and found that one of the subject headings for this book was 'Fisheries – North Atlantic Ocean – Congresses'. (In some libraries the subject would be encoded as a number.) The subject heading suggested that a subject search under 'fisheries' would be more sensible than my earlier search under 'fishing'. Similarly, if the library uses a numerical subject classification, you might decide to search for all the books that share a particular class-mark.

   3. Subject: fisheries   1323 records
   4. Restrict search 3 by subject:
      mammals   2 records

Search 4 takes the results of search 3 and searches within them for books with a subject heading of 'mammals' to find books that have both 'fisheries' and 'mammals' among the subject headings. One of the two books found was the conference proceedings already described and the other was called *Marine Mammals and Fisheries* (Beddington *et al.* 1995).

This second book had as one of its subject headings 'Fisheries – environmental aspects', which seemed interesting; so finally, I searched under 'fisheries – environmental aspects'.

   5. Subject: fisheries – environmental
      aspects   13 records

These provided a useful general background on the ecological effects of marine fishing, and complemented the two books already found that dealt specifically with fisheries and marine mammals. The entire search took under ten minutes.

☞ **Choosing useful search terms may take careful thought and several attempts**

Searching for papers involves much the same process, although the search is a bit more laborious than a book search. Electronic databases let you search for individual references or find papers according to subject, author and so on. Different libraries subscribe to different databases; once again, the librarian is the person to ask about how to search the resources available in your library. The example below describes a search for papers about advances in our knowledge of the structure of ribosomes over the past few years, and how those advances have helped us to understand the mechanism of translation. The databases searched were Medline and Biological Abstracts for the years since 2001. A useful technique when looking for papers is to start with a fairly broad search and narrow it until the number of papers is manageable.

1. Search term: ribosome   4965 records
2. Restrict search 1 by paper type: review   157 records
3. Restrict search 2 by search term: structure   48 records
4. Restrict search 3 by search term: translation   25 records

Again, the successive restrictions ensure that papers will be found only if they are reviews with all the search terms 'ribosome', 'structure' and 'translation'. A quick look through the titles of these twenty-five enables us to choose a few, depending on our particular interest.

It is generally a good idea to be quite ruthless in order to narrow the result to five or ten articles. Finding a paper in the library or on the web and reading it thoroughly takes quite a lot of time. On the other hand, if there is anything crucial that you discard when pruning the results, it is likely to be cited as a reference in at least one of the papers that you end up with. Thus, the system of references provides an automatic safeguard against missing something vital. Since one paper leads to another, it generally makes sense to discard articles at the outset because you will probably get another chance to find them later on through chasing up references. The exception to this is if you want to be as certain as possible that you have covered everything, for example if you are writing a review.

☞ Searches should be restricted to a manageable number of papers

Knowing where a paper has been published does not guarantee easy access to it. Some of the material you come across in references will not be stocked by your library. There are two ways round this: either ignore the paper and make do with the ones in the library, or try to find the paper you need somewhere else. If the paper is sufficiently important to the topic you are investigating, you may feel that a search in other libraries is justified.

The search facilities available to you will again depend on the library, but there are databases that enable you to search for institutions that hold a particular journal, and many libraries are prepared, for a small fee, to send copies of articles to other libraries. The database WorldCat, for example, amalgamates tens of millions of entries from hundreds of library catalogues so that you can find all the institutions that carry a given title. A large number of libraries also offer online public-access catalogues (OPACs). The organisation HERO (Higher Education and Research Opportunities in the United Kingdom) has an extensive list of links to the OPACs of UK academic libraries, and some others, at <http://www.hero.ac.uk/uk/reference_and_subject_resources/ institution_facilities/online_catalogues_alphabetic3793.cfm>; extensive worldwide resources are available by following links from the same site.

Looking into the future

One of the limitations of references is that an article can, of course, only refer to pieces published before it: a paper can look only into its past. This certainly has its uses: references fill you in on anything you missed in the original literature search, expand the scope of that search and give detail on areas on which you want to focus. However, it would also be useful to be able to look into a paper's future and see what became of a given experiment or a line of reasoning after it had been published.

There is an ingenious database that does just that. The Science Citation Index (SCI) allows searches by citation: you put in a reference and the Index finds all the subsequent papers that cite it. For example, the 1993 paper by Reiter *et al.* describes an *Arabidopsis* mutant with altered cell walls. I wondered whether anyone had made the step from characterising mutants to cloning genes involved in polysaccharide synthesis, so I did an SCI search on Reiter's paper. The search revealed that 111 other papers had cited Reiter *et al.*, and it did not take long to look through their titles. Sure enough, several of the papers reported the cloning and characterisation of genes involved in the synthesis of sugars.

By combining searches that move backwards and forwards in time, we can build up a good enough background knowledge to embark on reading a research paper in detail.

Summary

- Research papers assume that you understand why a topic is of current interest and that you understand the background science.
- Textbooks are helpful for general scientific background. It is worth getting to know a few favourites.
- Review articles give a summary of recent ideas and experimental findings in a specific field.
- Original research articles are useful for finding detailed information. It is worth getting to know a few favourite journals.
- Library catalogues and bibliographical resources allow electronic searches for books and papers.
- Search terms must be carefully chosen. Do not worry if this takes some time and several attempts – it is time well spent.

REFERENCES

Alkire, L.G., Jr. (ed.) (1969; 15th edn 2004) *Periodical Title Abbreviations*, Detroit; London: Thomson Gale.

Beddington, J.R., Beverton, R.J.H. and Lavigne, D.M. (eds) (1985) *Marine Mammals and Fisheries*, London: G. Allen & Unwin.

Blix, A.S., Walløe, L. and Ulltang, Ø. (eds) (1995) *Whales, Seals, Fish and Man: Proceedings of the International Symposium on the Biology of Marine Mammals in the North East Atlantic, Tromsø, Norway, 29 November–1 December 1994*, Amsterdam: Elsevier.

<http://darwin.nmsu.edu/~molbio/bioABACUShome.htm> last accessed 5 December 2005

<http://www.hero.ac.uk/uk/reference_and_subject_resources/institution_facilities/online_catalogues_alphabetic3793.cfm> last accessed 5 December 2005

2

Medium and message

The papers discussed in this book were published in peer-reviewed journals. Peer review is the gold standard of scientific credibility. Like any other quality control process, it has its benefits and its limitations.

Peer review

What exactly happens to an article once it is submitted to a journal?

The answer depends on the journal and on the type of article. Certain journals have an editorial board to assess manuscripts, and will publish any submission that meets criteria for relevance, interest, originality and so on. Non-peer-reviewed writing can be outstanding – think of any piece of excellent journalism, a first-rate textbook or a dazzling conference talk. However, because of the many difficulties inherent in doing science and writing it up – difficulties discussed in the coming chapters – research articles that have not been rigorously and critically reviewed by experts are not considered to have the same scientific authority as those that have.

Most scholarly journals use the initial editorial review to eliminate a large proportion of submissions, but then send the most suitable-looking manuscripts to be reviewed by the author's peers – other experts in similar fields. Reviewers are supposed to engage in exactly the kind of active and critical reading that this book promotes. They then write reports on the manuscript, highlighting its strengths and weaknesses and often suggesting revisions. Manuscripts are typically sent to about three independent reviewers, who return their reports to the editor. Reviewers' comments are passed, usually anonymously, to authors, who have a chance to adapt their papers accordingly and to comment on the reviewers' reports.

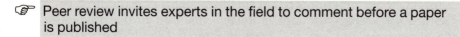 Peer review invites experts in the field to comment before a paper is published

Remember that not all the articles in peer-reviewed ('refereed') journals are subject to review. Non-refereed articles may include

- news
- editorials
- opinion pieces
- commissioned reviews of a field
- letters to the editor, for example critiques of other people's work.

These pieces of writing, on the whole, are more likely to be coloured by individual authors' opinions than refereed papers. This fact does not make such writing useless; on the contrary, it can be very instructive to read a discussion by scientists about the merits or otherwise of a published paper. On the other hand, opinion pieces have not been subjected to the same scrutiny as refereed research papers and subject reviews. The editorials quoted on pages 31 and 32 show some of the reasons that caution is necessary.

If a paper has already been 'passed' by a panel of experts, then why bother to read it actively yourself? Surely you can rely on the experts' imprimatur? Before you decide to ignore the advice in the rest of this book, let us look at some of the limitations of peer review.

Reviewing is a chore. Most researchers enjoy doing research. If they are asked to give up valuable time to review a manuscript, for little or more commonly no remuneration, they do not always respond with unbridled enthusiasm. Reviewing is a necessary part of the scholarly research process – and if I review a paper today I may expect my own manuscript to receive the same favour tomorrow – but it generally inspires a sense of duty more than a sense of glee. This is not to say that reviewers give the assignment short shrift. On the contrary, most reviewers, most of the time, approach the task extremely seriously and conscientiously. Nevertheless, the pressures on research scientists tend be dictated by their own research rather than by the needs of journals.

Reviewing can be difficult. One of the main ideas behind peer review is that researchers cannot always spot the flaws, ambiguities or loose ends in their own work. Inevitably, reviewers sometimes miss those shortcomings too. Godlee *et al.* (1998) deliberately introduced eight areas of weakness into a manuscript, and sent it to reviewers. Each reviewer spotted an average of two problems. Clearly, readers cannot sit back and assume that all the work of critical reading has been done for them before the paper is published.

Reviewers do not have the last word. The content of a journal is determined by its editors. Reports from reviewers are advisory, and editors have no obligation to accept them. Editors, as well as being scientific gatekeepers, are also intimately involved in the production of a commercial product, and have an interest in publishing exciting or revolutionary papers. Of course, no editor likes to be caught out by accepting a paper which later turns out to be unsound; nevertheless, the advice of cautious referees may not always be given the weight it deserves. Several people have spoken off the record about situations where they recommended strongly against publication of a manuscript that they reviewed, only to find themselves overruled by editors.

☞ **Peer-reviewed papers are favoured, but need careful reading anyway**

Some scientists have pointed out another feature of peer review: it tends to favour orthodoxies. Papers expressing a maverick opinion may be dismissed by conservative reviewers as madcap ramblings. This feature has led some researchers to claim that the scientific establishment is conspiring to keep out findings that challenge the tyranny of the status quo. While I think such claims are seriously exaggerated, it is also true that, as we have seen, peer review is far from being a perfect process.

Prestige or puff?

We all know that some journals are more highly respected and more prestigious than others. Respect for a journal is based on its record for editorial judgement and integrity and the rigour of its papers. Prestige is based on a journal's reputation for being the place where the most brilliant research appears. While these two attributes are certainly linked, they are not identical. Scientists may describe a journal as being *the* place to publish even as they acknowledge that it tries a bit too hard, sometimes at the expense of measured deliberation, to make a splash.

One way of assessing the quality of a publication is through its Impact Factor®, which looks at how often it is cited in other papers. The idea is that if a journal's recent articles are cited frequently on average, the journal must presumably be carrying important work. The system is of course not sophisticated enough to give any absolute indication of journal quality on its own. For one thing, the calculation is open to artefacts. For example, review articles tend to be cited frequently, so if a journal carries a lot of reviews compared to research papers, it is likely to be cited a lot. Furthermore, unmoderated calculations of citation frequency are open to abuse, with people having an incentive to cite their own or their friends' papers more than strictly necessary. More sophisticated methods are increasingly being used to judge the impact of journals or of individual articles.

One unsophisticated but useful way to assess journal quality is to ask research scientists themselves. That way, you can find out your colleagues' views on 'respected' and 'prestigious' journals. You can seek similar opinions about which individual scientists or laboratories are known for meticulous work and which are inclined to hype.

THE INTERNET AND OTHER SOURCES

A tangled web

The problem of variable quality is pronounced on the internet, where there is very little quality control. Of course, this caveat does not apply to online versions of peer-reviewed print journals. Many online-only journals are also peer reviewed; follow the journal's link to 'further information' or 'information for authors', and you will find a description of the journal which should indicate whether it is refereed. A welcome development in online publishing is the open-access journal. The publishing company BioMed Central <http://www.biomedcentral.com>, for example, produces over 100 online, peer-reviewed journals with access freely available to all. It remains to be seen whether such ventures will acquire a reputation comparable with that of the best printed journals.

The web is useful not just for consulting refereed publications but also for finding background information on unfamiliar topics. Online encyclopaedias and university lecture notes can both be helpful. One of the examples in Chapter 1 involved genetic complementation. Web searches for explanations provided by educational sites produce thousands of hits. Here is a definition provided in an online textbook belonging to the Massachusetts Institute of Technology (<http://web.mit.edu/esgbio/www/pge/comp.html>).

When we study . . . genetics, we often randomly mutagenize [organisms] and look for mutants that are deficient in the process that we're studying. If we generate many mutants, how do we tell how many of them are mutated in the same gene, and how many different genes there are? One method is to do a complementation test. If two [individuals] are crossed to each other, and each is mutated in the same gene, function will not be restored. On the other hand, if the mutations are in different genes, then the good copy of each gene in the other [individual] will fulfill the function of the mutated gene, or **complement** it . . . [The diagram represents a complementation test in bacterial cells:]

Medium and message

Given two genes necessary for the synthesis of arginine
The following diploids are made:

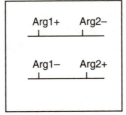
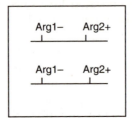

This cell has at least one
functional copy of each
gene, so it can make its
own arginine.

This cell has no functional
copies of Arg1, so it will
not be able to grow unless
supplemented with arginine.

Thus, Arg1 mutants could complement Arg2 mutants, but Arg1
mutants cannot complement themselves.

Figure 2.1 Complementation test in bacterial cells, from MIT online textbook.
(© Massachusetts Institute of Technology 2001. Used with permission.)

If we generate a lot of mutants and cross them all with each other, we
can discover a series of **complementation groups**; that is, mutants whose
mutations do not complement each other and are thus in the same gene.
[The web page provides an example].

This explanation is clear and accurate. Taken together, the text and the
diagram give a good picture of how the test is performed and how
it works. The website carefully defines the terms 'complementation'
and 'complementation group'. The trouble is that you might instead
have found this offering on a page belonging to another American
university:

Occasionally, multiple mutations of a single wild type phenotype are
observed. The appropriate genetic question to ask is whether any of the
mutations are in a single gene, or whether each mutations represents
one of the several genes necessary for a phenotype to be expressed. The
simplest test to distinguish between the two possibilities is the **complementation test**. The test is simple to perform – two mutants are crossed,
and the F1 is analyzed. If the F1 expresses the wild type phenotype, we
conclude each mutation is in one of two possible genes necessary for
the wild type phenotype. When it is shown that shown genetically that
two (or more) genes control a phenotype, the genes are said to form a
complementation group. Alternatively, if the F1 does not express the
wild type phenotype, but rather a mutant phenotype, we conclude that
both mutations occur in the same gene.

The conclusion – that restoration of the wild-type phenotype indicates
that the mutations are in different genes, while the failure to restore
wild-type phenotype shows that the mutations are in the same gene –

is correct. However, the wording is misleading. The website mentions 'the several genes necessary for a phenotype to be expressed', and in particular 'two possible genes necessary for the wild type phenotype'. Many genes are of course needed to maintain the wild-type phenotype, but the important point here is that we are talking about a group of genes whose *mutations* lead to *the same abnormal phenotype*. Even more problematically, the web page defines a complementation group as a set of genes that between them control a phenotype, as distinct from a set of mutations in one gene. In fact, a complementation group is exactly the opposite: a set of mutations that *fail* to complement each other and hence are in the *same* gene. A paper discussing the results of complementation experiments will thus use 'complementation group' more or less synonymously with 'gene'. If you were relying on the above definition, you would be likely to find such a paper confusing.

Useful questions to consider for any online resource are

- who wrote the material?
- for whom is it intended?
- is it referenced or attributed in a scholarly way?
- is it dated so that you can tell whether the information is current?

Regardless of the source of a web page, it is sensible to verify anything you find on the internet. The problem of inaccuracies, incidentally, exists to some extent in printed textbooks too. However, because web pages do not usually undergo the same editorial process as books, the risk is far greater with websites.

Copying errors

A risk that applies to both print and electronic media is the perpetuation of errors from source to source. Authors of textbooks must derive at least some of their information from other textbooks. Unfortunately, if the information is mistaken, the same error will creep into the new book. The same is even truer of websites, where there is more, and more direct, copying.

An interesting website is <http://bip.cnrs-mrs.fr/bip10/howler.htm>, whose author has collated several common errors that appear in many biochemistry textbooks. The site is in need of updating but gives a good illustration of how errors can be perpetuated.

For an online example, take the following quotations from three websites:

'Animal cloning has been the subject of scientific experiments for years. [The website discusses the cloning of a frog embryo in the 1950s]. . .. Animal cloning had little attention until the birth of the first cloned mammal in 1997, a sheep named Dolly.' (*From a community college website.*)

'Animal cloning has been the subject of scientific experiments for years, but garnered little attention until the birth of the first cloned mammal in 1997, a sheep named Dolly.' (*From an educational media website.*)

'Animal cloning has been the subject of scientific experiments for years, but has drawn little attention until the birth of the first cloned mammal in 1997, a sheep named Dolly.' (*From a website offering free essays for students.*)

Of course, these three sites may have chosen similar forms of words entirely independently. The main point of this example is that Dolly, the cloned sheep born in 1996 (whose birth was announced in 1997), was not the first cloned mammal. Although she was the first to be cloned from an adult somatic cell, scientists had been cloning mammals since at least the mid-1980s from cells taken from early embryos, and in 1995 two cloned sheep were produced from cultured embryonic cells.

 Websites need particularly careful scrutiny

Summary

- Scholarly journals subject manuscripts to peer review, allowing experts to comment on a paper before it is published and to suggest alterations.
- Peer reviewers may miss shortcomings in manuscripts or may be overruled by journal editors.
- Research papers in scholarly journals are usually of high quality but, even in the most prestigious journals, are not infallible.
- Most of the internet is not quality controlled.
- Single unverified sources should not be relied on. Even claims that appear on many websites or in many textbooks are sometimes wrong.

REFERENCES

Godlee, F., Gale, C.R. and Martyn, C.N. (1998) 'Effect on the quality of peer review of blinding reviewers and asking them to sign their reports: a randomized controlled trial', *J. Amer. Med. Assoc.* 280: 237–40.

<http://bip.cnrs-mrs.fr/bip10/howler.htm> last accessed 5 December 2005.
<http://web.mit.edu/esgbio/www/pge/comp.html> last accessed 5 December 2005. The MIT hypertextbook as a whole is a large resource of somewhat variable quality, but the description of complementation is better than many I have seen.
<http://www.biomedcentral.com> last accessed 5 December 2005.

3

Scientists as authors

MacHine's hand shook slightly as he stirred his coffee. It was the third cup of the morning, yet he was still barely awake. Yesterday had been a bad day. The assay had been a dismal failure: test tubes littered the bench, unwashed; in the corner of the lab, the water bath gurgled forlornly. Gene had been at his bench till after midnight, trying to get the experiment to work. It was the last one, the one that would allow him to finish his results section, draw his final conclusions and send off the paper to the publisher. He tapped the spoon on the edge of the mug and laid it on a teetering pile of papers. Science was a struggle. But Gene knew that eventually he would succeed in rolling back the frontiers and a little bit more of the truth would be revealed.

TRUTH AND RELATIVE TRUTH

In many respects, Gene MacHine is a typical scientist. He is full of honest, earnest enthusiasm; his desire is to understand the world and all he cares about is getting an accurate result, no matter what that result might tell him.

A person like this ought to be an ideal writer of research papers. His papers should be clear, objective and unambiguous. His methods should be meticulous, his analysis impartial, his conclusions unassailable. Why then is the process of reading research papers rarely that simple?

In this chapter, we look at the nuanced world of real science. Thinking about the scientific research process as we read helps to remind us that science is not all black and white, and that subjective interpretation has a large part to play.

The world is orderly – isn't it?

It is easy to assume that one's chosen subject will yield a neat set of results, but research findings – especially in the life sciences – can be messy. As researchers know, an experiment that gives a positive result on Monday may be negative on Tuesday, and one is then left wondering whether either result was genuine. Even more commonly, results are not clear cut, so that today's run of an experiment may be strongly suggestive of a particular conclusion while tomorrow's run may be only mildly suggestive or neutral.

Papers in focus

The successful treatment of spinal cord injury is a holy grail of medical science. Injuries to the central nervous system or CNS – the brain and spinal cord – can have devastating effects, but the CNS is remarkably bad at regenerating itself. Imagine what a difference it would make to the lives of people with CNS injuries if they could be told, 'you'll be just fine in a few months' rather than, 'you'll never walk again'.

Certain proteins in the nervous system inhibit nerve growth. In a stable system, this is desirable: once the CNS is fully developed it should stop growing. However, the same proteins may also prevent the tissue from healing itself if it is injured. What if the production of the inhibitory proteins could be switched off? Would damaged spinal cords be able to repair themselves by sprouting new axons across the lesion? Three papers published together in the journal *Neuron* looked at mice that had been mutated in order to disrupt genes encoding the proteins Nogo-A, Nogo-B and Nogo-C, which inhibit nerve regeneration. The researchers cut the spinal cords of the mutant mice and looked at whether they recovered any better than normal mice.

Kim, J.-E., Li, S., GrandPré, T., Qiu, D. and Strittmatter, S.M. (2003) 'Axon regeneration in young adult mice lacking Nogo-A/B', *Neuron* 38: 187–99.

This paper found extensive growth of axons in part of the spinal cord after injury. The finding was not confined to microscopic examination of mouse tissue – mice also recovered at least some movement:

> Overall, long-distance axonal regeneration is prominent in a majority of the *nogo-A/B$^{-/-}$* mice examined . . . the locomotor recovery in the *nogo-A/B$^{-/-}$* mice is significantly greater than in control mice.

The next paper in the same issue deals with essentially the same subject.

Simonen, M., Pedersen, V., Weinmann, O., Schnell, L., Buss, A., Ledermann, B., Christ, F., Sansig, G., van der Putten, H. and Schwab, M.E. (2003) 'Systemic deletion of the myelin-associated outgrowth inhibitor Nogo-A improves regenerative and plastic responses after spinal cord injury', *Neuron* 38: 201–11.

This paper found some axon growth in the mutated mice:

The results show that following dorsal transection lesions of the adult spinal cord, plastic and regenerative processes in Nogo-A ablated mice are improved compared to wild-type littermates.

However, the effect was less than that found in the previous paper, and no improvement in locomotor activity was reported.

A third paper took an independent look at the same question.

Zheng, B., Ho, C., Li, S., Keirstead, H., Steward, O. and Tessier-Lavigne, M. (2003) 'Lack of enhanced spinal regeneration in Nogo-deficient mice', *Neuron* 38: 213–24.

Unlike the other two groups, these scientists found no effect of mutating *nogo* genes on either the regrowth of injured neurons *in vivo* or the locomotor abilities of injured mice:

There was no indication of a greater degree of regeneration or sprouting in the Nogo-A/B mutant animals . . . there was no statistically significant difference between the mutants and wild-type animals in the degree of functional recovery . . .

It is difficult to account for the remarkable divergence between our study and [that of Kim *et al.*, the first example given above].

This set of papers makes fascinating reading and raises interesting questions. In the first place, why were the observations so different in the three laboratories? The authors (one of whom appears on two of the papers) make some attempt to explain the discrepancy in terms of the genetic backgrounds of the mouse strains and the possible interactions of the *nogo* genes with other, unknown genetic factors. However, it is clear that none of the groups has any very specific idea what is going on: the topic is simply at too early a stage of study. Second, how have the papers contributed to knowledge about nerve regeneration? All of them certainly contain interesting and informative results apart from those that I have quoted. Yet concerning the specific question, 'Can Nogo-deficient mice recover from spinal cord injury better than normal mice?', we seem to be none the wiser. What the papers have done towards addressing this question is to clarify an area of ignorance and to develop systems (such as mutant strains and standardised experimental methods) that can be used to investigate it further.

☞ **It is helpful to think about how research really works as you read**

It is noteworthy that these three groups of researchers decided to share their results and publish them together, with full references to each other. It would help readers if this were done more frequently, and these groups have done science a service by pooling their findings before publication. The discrepancies in the results are not due to any obvious deficiency in research methodology or interpretation; they simply reflect the difficulty of the experiments and the impossibility of controlling for every possible variable that might affect matters. Whether authors acknowledge it or not, conclusions at the vanguard of science are often tentative.

This uncertainty means that researchers need to be careful about how they replicate experiments and interpret their results. They need to decide what material is worthy of publication and which results should be omitted. With such a dependence on the choices of individual investigators, experimental science must give up any pretence to complete objectivity.

☞ Results can be untidy, so published papers must be selective

The criteria by which authors condense their results into publishable form are typically not explicit. Different researchers may have different practices and will be guided by different views about what they are trying to achieve and competing impulses as to how to go about it. If the biological world is not as orderly as we would like to think, how do Gene MacHine and others like him assess their own results before writing them up and submitting them for publication?

The usual way to understand experimental results is to measure them against a definite hypothesis. In fact, this is such a universal feature of doing science that it is easy to overlook its significance. We may like to think that scientists simply observe the real world with no prior expectation; but only newborn babies do that, and they do not make scientific breakthroughs.

It is impossible – and it would be nonsensical – to perform an experiment with a completely open mind. Often one expects a result such as 'a given quantity of this new antibiotic will kill at least 99.99% of my bacterial sample'. Even when the expectation is not so definite, one expects *something*, perhaps along the lines of 'either this chemical has an effect on bacterial growth – in which case the effect should be consistent – or it has no effect'.

Imagine that you test this hypothesis by plating bacteria onto agar plates laced with the chemical to be tested for antibiotic properties. Suppose that no bacteria grow on one of the plates, while on a second plate, several colonies grow. You may rationalise, 'the compound has some effect on bacterial growth, but the effect is very variable.' On the other hand, maybe you think, 'the compound prevents bacterial growth, but for some reason it did not work on one of the plates – perhaps there were some resistant bacteria or the chemical was not spread through the plate.' Or perhaps you conclude, 'the compound does not have any effect, but for some reason the bacteria did not grow on one of the plates – maybe they were killed by the heat I used to sterilise my equipment between plates.'

Real examples are usually rather more subtle. A typical scenario is one in which a researcher cannot explain a rogue result other than by assuming (for example) that one of the samples was contaminated. In this case, the result concerned will very likely be dismissed as an artefact and omitted from the published paper. But how can the researcher be sure that contamination really was the problem? Was this a mere artefact, or was it a genuine observation that needs to be explored further? Real experiments often generate inconsistencies that need explaining. Researchers' expectations as to what will happen, and their ideas about what factors may be complicating things, will affect the way in which they select, interpret and portray their results. Hypotheses form the lenses through which results are viewed.

 Authors' preconceptions influence their interpretation of results

Artefact or ugly fact?

What Thomas Huxley called 'the great tragedy of Science – the slaying of a beautiful hypothesis by an ugly fact' is a necessary tragedy if science is to progress. Without slaying incorrect hypotheses, scientists could not build better ones. However, it may be painful to kill off a theory that has been developed and worked on for a long time, and it is often easier to interpret ambiguous results in such a way that bloodshed can be avoided.

An example concerns hypotheses for the mechanism of oxidative phosphorylation, that is, the synthesis of ATP from ADP and inorganic phosphate in mitochondria. The question was how the energy released from the breakdown of nutrients is used to drive the phosphorylation reaction. The biochemist E.C. Slater (1953) proposed a 'chemical hypothesis' whereby an enzyme in the mitochondrion reacts with a chemical intermediate to form a high-energy compound, which in turn releases the energy needed to synthesise ATP from ADP and phosphate.

A serious drawback of this idea was that nobody could find the high-energy intermediates that Slater proposed. Some years later, Peter Mitchell (1961) put forward an alternative 'chemi-osmotic' hypothesis. According to Mitchell, the energy produced by the breakdown of nutrients was used to transport protons across the mitochondrial membrane, creating potential energy in the form of a proton gradient. The energy could be released by allowing the protons to flow back across the membrane at another site, where ATP could be synthesised.

Slater, whose idea was conceptually attractive and firmly based on principles known from other biochemical systems, did not accept the Mitchell hypothesis right away. He was still proposing a role for high-energy intermediates in 1970 (Slater *et al.* 1970; this is a short paper that makes no reference to Mitchell), although there was no direct proof of their existence. But some years later, Slater was to write, 'The three formulations [of the mechanism] have been put alongside one another in Figure 3; the so-called chemical hypothesis is included only for historical reasons and in order to state that it is now untenable' (Boyer *et al.* 1977). For someone who had seen his beautiful theory overthrown, this was a remarkably gracious retraction.

The story does not end there: when later developments called into question some of Mitchell's ideas, he too was apparently slow to accept the required modifications to his theory (Slater 2003). In fact, a certain amount of resistance to new ideas is probably one of the universal features of the way that science is done. This is just as well: it would be absurd if every one-off unexpected result precipitated a scientific revolution and an abandonment of established theories.

☞ Authors' backgrounds and points of view influence their writing

For us as readers, this means that we need to familiarise ourselves with a field as much as possible before interpreting novel research findings. We need to ask whether a paper is in line with conventional thinking or whether it represents a departure from the accepted view. We need to ask who the authors are and whether they may have any particular axe to grind. The best way to do this is to discuss papers with active researchers in the field.

The process of authorial interpretation is not some sinister plot to distort the truth or to uphold a theory that experiments have falsified. The point is that experimental results often admit of more than one interpretation. Any of several interpretations might be equally sound from a scientific point of view, and all of them might entail giving some results more weight than others. Frequently, the interpretation that upholds a tried and tested theory will be the correct one. Sometimes it will not. But any author's choice of interpretation is bound to be somewhat subjective.

INTERPRETATION AND PRESENTATION

The difficulty of producing clear and reproducible results makes it important for readers to be alert. There are other factors that also influence the kinds of papers that are written and published and the way in which they are written, making the reader's input even more crucial.

The academic funding crisis

Science is an expensive business. Experiments require facilities such as lab space, animal houses and field stations; equipment like freezers, centrifuges and microscopes; and a wide range of consumables. Getting grants to pay for all these is a highly competitive enterprise. For many academic researchers, their salaries are also dependent on grants.

Naturally, any grant-giving body will want to be satisfied that its money is being well spent. And so, naturally, scientists will be required to give an account of themselves to their paymasters. Failure to publish, or to publish enough papers in sufficiently prestigious journals, may mean that a researcher's funding dries up right in the middle of a project. All this is quite reasonable in principle, but it would be surprising if scientists could completely avoid putting a favourable spin on their work when so much is at stake.

University departments as well as individual researchers must compete for funding and, as scientists know, public funding of universities is limited. Increasingly, researchers need to rely on finding other sources of funding through, for example, philanthropic donations or collaborations with industry. Businesses are no more willing to waste money than funding councils, and academic scientists who wish to attract external funding must portray their work as being worth the money. Furthermore, there may be several angles to a scientist's work, and the one that is stressed may depend on the source of funding that is being approached. For example, work on the way in which cells communicate with each other could be relevant to cancer, immunology or fertility research, and the same piece of work could be described in one way when making a grant application to a cancer charity and in another way when pitching to a pharmaceutical company that makes drugs for treating infertility. The source of funding may then go on to determine the way in which the work is written up and published in journal articles. There may be a rush to publish before the next grant application needs to go in, or a tendency to stress certain aspects of the work at the expense of others. Concerns about funding will affect the text that a reader of papers has to deal with.

☞ The need to attract and maintain funding can influence authors' presentation

As with selecting and rationalising results, there is not necessarily anything untoward or dishonest about presenting them in a particular way. On the other hand, just as readers must understand how researchers select results and draw conclusions, so must they understand the pressures on researchers to put a certain gloss on their work. Readers must ask themselves whether a paper has been published before it is really ready, and whether this means that some of the results are less reliable than they might be. For example, a 1999 paper in the *European Journal of Neuroscience* contains the phrase '[the work] of others REFERENCE?'. Clearly, an incomplete draft of the paper has been published. Is this a single careless slip, where the authors left in the word 'REFERENCE?' rather than finding the actual reference and citing it; or were the authors or the journal in too much of a hurry? Most likely the former – it is easy to make one error in an otherwise excellent paper – but it is the reader's responsibility to decide.

Science meets business

Funding is a problem for commercial laboratories as well as academic ones, but the response to the problem is rather different in the two sectors. In a pharmaceutical company, for example, income is measured in drug sales and financial standing typically in terms of share price. Sales rely on past research and development success; share prices depend on predictions of future success; and both are affected by the activities of competitors. How do these specific pressures affect the publications coming out of commercial research laboratories?

A university scientist who discovers a result with no obvious commercial application is likely to want to publish it sooner rather than later. On the other hand, an industrial research scientist must consider how to protect intellectual property if it is commercially valuable. Protection entails either lodging a patent application – which may take months – or keeping an invention secret. Publishing immediately in a journal, and sharing unprotected results with competitors, is ruled out. The commercial sector thus has a built-in incentive not to publish results. We should also remember that academics are usually free to publish with the approval of an immediate boss, while large companies can be expected to vet every paper at a senior level before allowing it to be submitted for publication.

When we read industry papers that *have* found their way into journals, it therefore makes sense to ask 'why did they publish this now?', whereas for academic papers, the question is frequently a non-issue. The distinction between commerce and academe is not clear-cut: universities produce commercially sensitive results that must be safeguarded before publication, and industry produces results that it is eager to share right away. However, on the whole, the pressures we have already discussed are enough to justify an academic publication, whereas for a commercial publication additional motives are often needed to overcome the pressures against publishing.

 Commercial publications raise their own questions

One such motive is the ending of a project. So long as an avenue of research looks exciting and commercially promising, it is probably a good idea not to tell too many people about it. Once a project dries up and is shelved, it stops generating tomorrow's sales hopes and starts supplying today's column inches. The same is true of projects that made good progress and produced interesting results, but that the company has decided to drop for strategic reasons.

A paper or a series of papers on a similar topic from a commercial lab can thus provide a clue that the project is no longer active. Confusingly, a paper may also provide a clue that the project is going well and that the company wishes to pique interest in a forthcoming product. There is no way of telling for sure, but familiarity with individual laboratories and with the progress of research in individual companies can help you to guess.

Familiarity with labs and scientists can also help you to guess something about a laboratory's current work from its recent publications. Journals should publish the date on which a manuscript was first received, and that will give you some idea of how far the work is likely to have progressed since then. What you do not see is the date on which the work was actually done. Reading a paper from industry thus raises three intriguing possibilities: either the work is old and defunct and has been published to put worthwhile science into the public domain or even to mislead competitors; or the results are a bit stale and the project has advanced far beyond what is revealed in the paper; or the work is up to date and exciting and has been rushed into print in order to gain kudos for the laboratory. Some of these possibilities are far more likely to pertain to commercial than to academic labs. There is no simple set of rules to distinguish them; as is so often the case, the clues are best detected by a practised eye.

Stockholm beckons

The financial reward of a successful grant application is not the only incentive for university scientists. Like any other group of people, scientists will vary in their personalities and motives. Some will be very ambitious, others less so. Some will be keen to build CV points and to apply for new jobs, others will be content to stay where they are but may work flat out to secure tenure. Almost all will get a buzz from an exciting result, otherwise they would not be doing the work they do.

Ambition tends to impel scientists towards publishing as many papers as possible and/or publishing in the most prestigious journals possible. The desire to get multiple papers out of a single set of results can tempt authors to 'sausage-slice' their work into fragments jokingly referred to as MPUs – minimum publishable units. A piece of work that is quite extensive but not good enough for a paper in the most competitive journals may be written up in a second-tier journal – as two papers. Better still, the papers may cite each other, an advantage for authors since one rough-and-ready way of assessing the importance of a paper is to count the number of other papers that cite it as a reference.

Imagine the thrill of making a major breakthrough – a vaccine against HIV, for example, or a cure for a certain cancer. Journals would be clamouring to publish one's results. Recognition would be assured, of a degree corresponding to the importance of the result. For some, it could mean a promotion; others might expect a national award; in some cases, even a Nobel prize would not be out of the question.

Most scientists are down to earth about how much excitement to expect during their careers; but many surely dream, once in a while, of achievement beyond the strictly realistic. Dreams make for progress and the genuine advancement of knowledge, and are certainly not to be decried. However, they may also make for over-optimistic descriptions or for premature publication. Ambitious scientists may be inclined to window-dress results so that they look exciting. Some of them may be inclined to forego a certain amount of critical evaluation where it will hold up publication of an article and allow a competitor to publish first. The outcome may be the opposite of the phenomenon described above, where researchers dismiss a genuine observation as a mistake. Here, they may be so elated to have 'discovered' something that they publish artefactual findings as real results. Truth is important, but personal achievement is also a great motivator.

☞ **Ambitious people may tend to exaggerate the significance of their work**

I do not suggest that any but a small minority of scientists value achievement above truth; merely that understandable pressures, such as the wish to make a useful contribution to science or medicine, or the desire for recognition, inevitably interpose a subjective step in the transfer of absolute truth – if there is such a thing – to the printed page.

Sex sells

Readers dream too. It is easy to be swept up in the enthusiasm of an author's writing and the landscape of possibility that it illuminates. But beware! A beautiful vista can be enticing – but is it genuine or merely a mirage? The more startling a result is, the more ideas and experiments it is likely to stimulate and the more tempting it is to take the paper at face value; but being exciting does not make a result right. It is important not to judge a paper on how important it would be if it were correct, but rather on how likely it is to be correct given the quality of the work.

This caveat applies not only to readers but to referees and journal editors too.

Paper in focus

Szuromi, P. (ed.) (1999) 'Histone phosphorylation', *Science* 285: 801.

The way in which gene expression is regulated is a central question in biology. Development proceeds by a series of decisions about switching genes on and off. The genomes of our close relatives, the great apes, are so similar to ours that many of the differences between the species are thought to reflect differences in gene expression rather than differences in gene sequences themselves. Cancer ultimately results from aberrant gene expression.

One factor influencing gene expression is the structure of chromatin, the DNA/protein complex of which chromosomes are made. For example, DNA tightly complexed with histone proteins is less likely to be accessible to transcription machinery than DNA associated only loosely with histones. The tightness of DNA–histone binding, and the accessibility of chromatin to other proteins, are affected by covalent modifications to the histone proteins themselves. Understanding these modifications is therefore a step towards understanding development and cancer. This editorial describes a paper in the same issue of *Science* about a type of histone modification.

> One way in which gene transcription can be regulated is through remodeling of chromatin structure. Histone proteins are known to be modified through acetylation and deacetylation by enzymes recruited to specific promoters. Sassone-Corsi *et al.* (p. 886) provide evidence that another modification of histones – covalent phosphorylation – may also contribute to growth factor-induced gene expression . . ..
> The findings raise the possibility that phosphorylation of histones could influence chromatin structure and thus be part of the mechanism by which EGF [epidermal growth factor] alters gene activation.

The journal is clearly excited by this paper: it records a significant discovery in a fashionable field, and that presumably is why it merited editorial comment. However, unlike the editorial, the paper itself does not suggest that histone phosphorylation and its effect on growth factor-induced gene expression are new discoveries, for the very good reason that they had been documented some years earlier in a paper from another laboratory (Mahadevan *et al.* 1991).

Paper in focus

Anonymous (1971) 'Lifting replication out of the rut', *Nature New Biology* 233: 97–8.

In the 1950s, a bacterial DNA polymerase was isolated by Arthur Kornberg, and was assumed to be the enzyme responsible for DNA replication. It was extensively studied in order to elucidate the mechanism of replication. However, a mutant was subsequently discovered that lacked the enzyme but could nonetheless replicate its DNA. The discovery prompted the search for new DNA polymerases, as it became clear that the Kornberg polymerase is a DNA repair enzyme rather than the DNA-replicating enzyme. Some scientists questioned whether the enzyme they were searching for would use the same mechanism as the repair enzyme. For example, they wondered whether the replicase would use deoxyribonucleoside triphosphates (dNTPs) as DNA precursors, as the Kornberg polymerase does, or whether it would use some other precursor. The former seemed more likely for biochemical and cell-biological reasons, but it had not been proven.

In this editorial, an anonymous writer describes new work published in the same issue of *Nature* suggesting that the replicating enzyme does not use dNTPs as precursors. The writer pours considerable scorn on much of the previous work, ignoring the sound biochemical reasons why most researchers assumed the precursors to be dNTPs – as we now know them to be:

> Although it is abundantly evident to the spectators and practitioners of molecular biology alike that precious little progress has been made in the past two decades towards elucidating the biochemistry of DNA replication, most researchers continue to travel hopefully along well worn paths and, not surprisingly, show few signs of reaching their declared destination. Having spent years trying to devise ingenious schemes to explain how DNA polymerase I, the enzyme Kornberg and his colleagues so remorselessly pursued (which, as is now known, has a repair function *in vivo* and is not involved in DNA replication), might replicate DNA, molecular biologists are apparently finding it hard to change their way of thinking about this problem. Group after group, in spite of knowing that polymerase I is a repair enzyme, have nevertheless been content to adopt Kornberg's assay systems in their search for DNA replicase. They have assumed without question that the replicase must use the four nucleoside triphosphates [sic] as precursors for DNA replication because polymerase I uses them as precursors for DNA repair synthesis.

And so on. Surely the reason why this editorial is so disparaging is not really because all previous researchers had been shoddy and had overlooked the obvious. Presumably it is because the journal was publishing a potentially exciting paper, and if the discovery of non-dNTP precursors had been correct it would have been surprising and important. It is for the reader to approach this kind of writing with caution, for nothing in the editorial itself alerts us to the fact that the published hypothesis actually turned out to be wrong.

☞ **Papers and editorials are not immune to journalistic rhetoric**

Nobody could expect editorial writers for journals as broad as *Science* or *Nature* to be experts in every field. Sometimes a reference will be overlooked, an existing body of literature tossed too lightly aside or an editorial neck stuck out too far. But you can be sure that glamorous papers attract more editorials – and more editorial hype – than others.

☞ **Papers that claim to overturn accepted norms need particular care**

INVISIBLE SCIENCE

So far we have discussed the need to be alert to influences on how results are selected, interpreted and written up. With published material in front of us, we can dissect and analyse what scientists have said and reach conclusions about the suitability of their methods, the reliability of their results and the plausibility of their interpretations. Much of the time, readers can admire the care with which the experiment has been carried out and reported. Some of the time, we may conclude that it is too early to make a definite statement and that further work is required. On occasion we might spot flaws, ambiguities or omissions.

In this section, we discuss why some results get into print, not through being correct but simply because they are the right kind of results; and we look at influences that conspire to keep other results unpublished. When we read material suggesting a particular conclusion, we should remember that equally sound results suggesting another conclusion may lurk out of sight.

Publication bias and reference bias

'Mitochondrial dysfunction in the elderly: no apparent role in insulin resistance.' 'Light quality has no effect on flowering time.' 'No particular benefit from cholesterol-lowering in patients with diabetes.'

A glance at these spurious headlines makes it obvious why journals prefer to publish positive results (ones that demonstrate the existence of a phenomenon) rather than negative ones (results showing that something is not the case). In fact, the misquotations are based on real articles published in *Science*, *Nature* and *The Lancet* in 2003 – but the original titles introduce articles that make a positive claim (for example 'Regulation of flowering time by light quality'). Negative results simply do not sell journals, unless they contradict a well-established belief or relate to an area of particular interest or controversy. Negative results often seem unexciting to their discoverers too, and may not even be submitted for publication.

The well-established tendency of journals to prefer positive results to negative ones is an example of publication bias, and it can distort scientific understanding. Suppose that I test a popular dietary supplement for its benefit in preventing heart attacks, and discover that it is harmless but completely ineffective. Should not doctors and patients be informed? If there is a particular interest in the supplement as a possible heart remedy and my study is topical, perhaps a journal will accept my report; otherwise I may well struggle to find a publisher. A potentially important piece of knowledge will remain hidden.

The situation is the same in pure science. Take the first title as an example. If I studied the influence of mitochondrial dysfunction on insulin resistance and found no effect, I would not be surprised if my paper were turned down by a journal, and might quite likely not bother trying to get it published in the first place. Yet the consequent invisibility of my results could have profound repercussions. Another scientist – or several groups of scientists – might waste time, effort and resources studying the same question and coming to the same negative conclusion. This is an especially serious problem when human subjects, laboratory animals, or large investments are involved.

Alternatively, another scientist might perform a similar experiment and find that mitochondrial dysfunction *does* have a role in insulin resistance. If that experiment is published, then it will become the last word on the subject, unquestioned and unreplicated. What if it flies in the face of a hundred sets of discarded results suggesting the contrary? What if the published result is an error, or applies only to a small subset of patients?

This example may rather stretch the point, but there is an important point to be made. Results at the vanguard of science may be controversial or uncertain. You should not assume that every piece of research in the field agrees with the one that you are reading about. The mere fact that something has been published does not make it so; and the 'ordinariness' of negative results means that the published information in a field may be biased towards the positive – including false positives.

Even where authors know of results contradicting their findings, they may on occasion conveniently forget to draw attention to them. It is far simpler to be able to say, 'eating fish oil is good for you' than to have to say, 'our experiment suggests a possible benefit, but the meticulous work of Bloggs and Doe (2005) failed to find any beneficial effect, so we might be wrong.' Not only is omitting ifs and buts simple, it also increases the apparent impact of a paper, which is useful for authors. If a result appears too tentative, journals may be reluctant to publish it.

An extreme example of this kind of problem can be found in a pair of 1978 papers concerning an enzyme whose level in the blood is lower in schizophrenics than in people without schizophrenia. The research was important because it was relevant to attempts to diagnose schizophrenia accurately and early. A paper in the *New England Journal of Medicine* drew interesting conclusions. One of the main findings was that levels of the enzyme differed between paranoid and non-paranoid schizophrenics: the Abstract states, 'Chronic paranoid schizophrenics . . . differed significantly from chronic nonparanoid schizophrenics.' Almost simultaneously, a paper appeared in the *American Journal of Psychiatry*, investigating the same enzyme. The Abstract of this second paper states, 'There were no significant differences [in levels of the enzyme] in 21 chronic paranoid schizophrenic patients compared with 18 chronic undifferentiated schizophrenic patients.' Given what we know about the difficulty of reproducing results, and the difficulty of diagnosing schizophrenia and dividing patients into paranoid and non-paranoid groups, it is not all that surprising to find a contradiction between the two papers. Since they appeared at more or less the same time, it might not seem unusual that the papers make no mention of each other. However, a remarkable fact was noted by a correspondent to the *New England Journal*: the papers share two co-authors! Following a comment by the *Journal*'s editors (who declared themselves 'puzzled by . . . this bizarre event'), the authors expressed 'sincere regret' for not having mentioned their own discrepant results. They may have felt that to draw attention to the contradiction would show up the results as inconclusive and jeopardise publication of the manuscripts (see Kohn 1988 for references).

The problem of data concealment appears to be commoner than one might hope. Martinson *et al.* (2005) asked 7,760 US scientists whether they had personally engaged in various kinds of scientific misbehaviour during the previous three years. Of 3,247 respondents, 6% admitted failing to present data that contradicted their own previous research.

Perhaps even more common than deliberate concealment is ignorance or carelessness, where authors have simply not managed to keep up with what may be a huge body of literature in their field, and overlook other people's work that really ought to be cited. Either way, the effect will be to mislead the reader as to the firmness of the conclusions. The reader in turn must be aware of this possibility and bear in mind that what looks like a clear result may well not be the whole story.

 Published results may not represent the only opinion on a subject

Calling the tune

It goes without saying that one of the most significant influences on the answer to a scientific enquiry is the question asked. Nowhere is this more clearly revealed than in studies examining how outcomes of medical experiments depend on the source of research funding. A huge body of literature has grown up on this subject; reviews of the literature have been undertaken; and even these reviews have themselves been reviewed (Lexchin *et al.* 2003).

This corpus of analysis shows that research funded by pharmaceutical companies is more likely to produce results that favour the sponsor's product than research with other sources of funding. There are several possible explanations of this phenomenon. A cynic might guess that drug companies somehow sponsor deliberately shoddy research that is biased in favour of their products; but in fact, the methodology of industry-funded trials has been shown to be at least as sound as the methodology of other trials.

However, some crucial points are omitted from calculations of research quality. First, assessments do not take account of the question asked. Once an appropriate question has been formulated, the experiment may do a very good job of investigating it; but even the most reliable answer is not informative if the question was not appropriate. If I am testing the effectiveness of a new drug, I may ask, 'How does the drug compare to a placebo?' or I may ask, 'How does the drug compare to the best available existing treatment?' Clearly, testing a novel treatment against a placebo or against no therapy at all is more likely to give a positive result than testing it against the conventional treatment, which may already be very effective. One review found that a far higher proportion of industry-funded trials than publicly funded trials did indeed compare novel treatments with placebos or no therapy. Even if a new treatment is tested against an existing competitor, it is possible to improve the appearance of the new treatment by using too low or too high a dose of the competitor.

Second, publication bias may be more prominent for trials funded by drug companies than for those funded by other bodies. Industry-funded research as a whole is less likely to be published than research with other sources of funding; whether this tendency affects unfavourable papers disproportionately is for the most part an open question. However, there are documented cases of manufacturers attempting to suppress publication of results unfavourable to their products (see Lexchin *et al.* 2003, and references therein).

 It is always worth asking who funded the research

It is difficult to analyse selective or biased reporting, because we do not usually know what unpublished results exist that might cast doubt on the published material. However, Melander and his colleagues (2003) have managed to carry out such an analysis. They looked at studies of a type of antidepressant, both published and unpublished, submitted to the Swedish drug regulatory authority by pharmaceutical companies wanting approval for their drugs. Since drug companies are obliged to submit reports of all studies performed, whether or not they are favourable and whether or not they have been published, the authors assumed that they had an exhaustive set of reports. They then compared this exhaustive set with the publicly available reports on the same drugs.

The findings were very revealing. In many cases, studies that were favourable to the product were reported more than once, sometimes with no cross-referencing and no common author, giving the false impression that two independent studies had endorsed the drug. Frequently, results from several studies of a drug that had already appeared in stand-alone publications were pooled and published again. Sometimes the same pool of results was written up several times, again often without adequate cross-referencing. Large studies could be performed across multiple research centres, with data from those centres that gave a particularly favourable result being selected for publication. Half of the studies submitted to the regulator showed significantly beneficial effects for the test drug, while the other half did not; but over 90% of the favourable studies appeared as stand-alone publications, compared with under 30% of the less favourable studies.

 The source of research funding influences published research outcomes

The prism of scientific spin may reveal or obscure, clarify or distort, but we can be certain that it will be there, refracting the real world's ever-shifting complexities and uncertainties into orderly, publishable form.

Summary

- Experimental results in life sciences are often not clear-cut and call for interpretation.
- Decisions about the reliability and significance of results depend on researchers' background, preconceptions and opinions.
- The content of published material is inevitably coloured by the way it is presented. Factors influencing presentation include the author's desires to maintain funding and to discover something interesting or useful, and the journal's wish to publish exciting results.

- Not all experiments are published, even if they contain valid or important science. Biases on publication include an aversion to negative results, the wish to protect intellectual property, and the selection and presentation of results for commercial advantage.
- Readers need to think about the pressures on researchers and journals in order to interpret published papers effectively.

REFERENCES

Boyer, P.D., Chance, B., Ernster, L., Mitchell, P., Racker, E. and Slater, E.C. (1977) 'Oxidative phosphorylation and photophosphorylation', *Annu. Rev. Biochem.* 46: 955–1026.

Kohn, A. (1988) *False Prophets: Fraud and Error in Science and Medicine*, revised edn, Oxford: Basil Blackwell. The case described appears in Chapter 12.

Lexchin, J., Bero, L.A., Djulbegovic, B. and Clark, O. (2003) 'Pharmaceutical industry sponsorship and research outcome and quality: a systematic review', *BMJ* 326: 1167–70.

Mahadevan, L.C., Willis, A.C. and Barratt, M.J. (1991) 'Rapid histone H3 phosphorylation in response to growth-factors, phorbol esters, okadaic acid, and protein-synthesis inhibitors', *Cell* 65: 775–83.

Martinson, B.C., Anderson, M.S. and de Vries, R. (2005) 'Scientists behaving badly', *Nature* 435: 737–8.

Melander, H., Ahlqvist-Rastad, J., Meijer, G. and Beermann, B. (2003) 'Evidence b(i)ased medicine – selective reporting from studies sponsored by pharmaceutical industry: review of studies in new drug applications', *BMJ* 326: 1171–3.

Mitchell, P. (1961) 'Coupling of phosphorylation to electron and hydrogen transfer by a chemi-osmotic type of mechanism', *Nature* 191: 144–8.

Slater, E.C. (1953) 'Mechanism of phosphorylation in the respiratory chain', *Nature* 172: 975–8.

—— (2003) 'Metabolic gardening', *Nature* 422: 816–17.

Slater, E.C., Lee, C.P., Berden, J.A. and Wegdam, H.J. (1970) 'High-energy forms of cytochrome *b*', *Nature* 226: 1248–9.

4

The Abstract and Introduction

As the manuscript slid out of its brown envelope, Professor Stickler sighed. It was that MacHine fellow again. To be sure, his ideas were interesting enough; it was just that he had no idea how to do an experiment or how to write it up. It was not Professor Stickler's day. Her morning had been wasted on a completely fruitless departmental meeting; she had precisely one day left to write a talk for the Bermuda conference; and now this. She began to read . . .

Cancer Risk from Tastie Root Chips

Abstract
Cancer is one of the leading causes of death in the developed world, and dietary factors are believed to play a causative role in many forms of the disease. The tastie root (*Radiculum esculentum*) is a staple in much of Europe, and tastie root chips have recently gone on sale in the United States. We have detected the known mutagen radicullin in samples of supermarket tastie root chips. The rising consumption of tastie roots may present a hazard to public health in the USA. In addition, we propose that a decrease in the consumption of tastie roots in Europe could achieve a marked reduction in the European incidence of cancer.

Introduction
The tastie plant *Radiculum esculentum* was first described by the botanist Plantzman (1836). Its tuberous root is widely eaten in most European countries, where boiled tastie root accounts for a significant fraction of dietary carbohydrate (Eaton and Stuft, 1978). Although consumption of tastie root differs widely between countries, Bachov and Envelope (1994) estimated that, across the continent of Europe, average annual consumption amounts to approximately 48 kg per capita.

Tastie roots were unknown in the United States until the supermarket chain As-U-Like started marketing tastie root chips under the brand name Radichips in 1999. Since then, anecdotal evidence suggests that the product has grown rapidly in popularity.

Concern about the possible health effects of tastie roots recently surfaced with the discovery of a correlation between the estimated countrywide consumption of tastie root and the national death rates from liver cancer in seven European countries (Lyse, Damlise and Statz, 2001). Tastie plants have not until now been analysed for possible carcinogens. However, the related yukkie plant (*Radiculum foetidum*) has been extensively studied, and the most potent mutagen identified in that species is the heterocyclic amine radicullin discovered in a preparation of char-grilled yukkie root (Griddle and Byrne, 2002).

Because of the close genetic relationship between tastie and yukkie plants, we decided to test for the presence of radicullin in tastie root chips. Our findings have potentially grave implications for public health in the United States. We can now explain the correlation observed by Lyse *et al.* (2001), and suggest a simple expedient for remedying the alarming increase in the incidence of cancer across much of Europe.

FIRST IMPRESSIONS

This chapter is about two things. It is about the reasons why people read papers; and it is about using the opening sections of a paper to help you decide how to approach what follows. You may pick up a research report for all kinds of reasons, and it is as well to be clear what you want out of it before launching yourself into detailed reading.

Do I need to read the paper?

People read scientific publications for a variety of reasons. For example, you may read a paper

- for general interest or background information
- to find out exactly what the latest developments are in a field
- to seek evidence to support or refute your ideas
- to broaden your avenues of research
- to find out how a certain piece of research was done.

You may not know at the outset what you are going to use the paper for, and the Abstract and Introduction can help you to decide.

If you are writing a report on a subject, or if you need a general overview to inform your own research interests or to understand a seminar, you will probably want to read for background knowledge. In a large or fast-moving field, papers will be appearing as rapidly as you can keep up with them, and you will need to be selective about what to read. Reviews (see Chapter 1) are a useful place to start. Supervisors or colleagues with more experience in the field can help by suggesting important papers or researchers that they admire.

On the other hand, if you are embarking on experimental work in a specific area, you will need to be fully versed in the current state of knowledge. It will be important to read as widely as possible, not only about the background but also about the latest developments that might affect your work. The search strategies discussed in Chapter 1 will help you to locate a starting point. If you want to be really sure that you have covered all the relevant published work in the field, you will have to search quite exhaustively – and often exhaustingly. Spending a whole day searching for papers in the library can be pretty boring, certainly more so than querying a database for half an hour. Nevertheless, it is a very good investment if it will save you wasting six months on unnecessary experiments.

☞ *Why* you are reading determines *how* you should read

However you select a paper, the Abstract and Introduction should tell you whether it is worth reading in depth or only worth skimming. The answer will depend on what you are looking for. It is not a matter of finding 'good' papers and resolving to read them carefully, while relegating 'bad' papers to the *quick skim* pile. It is a matter of using the Abstract and Introduction in conjunction with your own research needs in order to plan a reading strategy.

Whatever your reason for reading, critical assessment of the paper is important. One useful trick is to read the experimental results – that is the figures and tables together with their legends – at least as closely as the main text. Another is to avoid reading the Discussion section until you have formulated your own ideas about the results and what they mean. It is quite easy to misinterpret or over-interpret an observation, so do not rely exclusively on the authors' views. Use your own judgement.

☞ Readers should evaluate results before reading the authors' conclusions

What is the paper about?

Science is about answers. A well-designed and truly scientific experiment addresses an issue of scientific concern, otherwise it becomes an exercise in speculative dabbling. Similarly, a well-written research report will clearly delineate the area under investigation. The places to find information about a paper's subject matter are the title, the Abstract and the Introduction. Sometimes, the Discussion contains further ideas, but it is not worth reading the Discussion in any detail until we have a good idea what is being discussed.

As we saw in Chapter 1, the Abstract is a brief statement of the results and conclusions of the paper, and is always a useful place to start. It is too short to contain a full description of the reasons behind the experiment, but authors will often include some pointers, which should be elaborated in the Introduction. Readers for their part should approach the Abstract with a question in mind: what controversy or orthodoxy does this research take as its starting point? Phrasing the question in this way does not imply that a raging argument lies behind every paper; it simply means that directed reading is far more productive than rambling reading, just as directed science is more productive than rambling science.

Paper in focus

Cui, T., Daniels, M., Wong, B.S., Li, R., Sy, M.-S., Sassoon, J. and Brown, D.R. (2003) 'Mapping the functional domain of the prion protein', *Eur. J. Biochem.* 270: 3368–76.

Prion diseases such as Creutzfeldt-Jakob disease are possibly caused by the conversion of a normal cellular glycoprotein, the prion protein (PrP^c) into an abnormal isoform (PrP^{Sc}). The process that causes this conversion is unknown, but to understand it requires a detailed insight into the normal activity of PrP^c. It has become accepted from results of numerous studies that PrP^c is a Cu-binding protein . . . .. Further work has suggested that PrP^c is an antioxidant . . . .. We have shown in this investigation that this activity is optimal for the whole protein and that deletion of parts of the protein reduce or abolish this activity. The protein therefore contains an active domain requiring certain regions . . . .. These regions show high evolutionary conservation fitting with the idea that they are important to the active domain of the protein.

This Abstract, together with the title, gives a very clear idea of why the research was done and what it has shown. The authors explain their interest in prions in terms of their medical importance, and go on to explain why it is necessary to clarify the function of the normal protein PrP^c. They give a succinct summary of their results, indicating what they have discovered about the functional domain of the protein and alluding to evidence from evolutionary studies in order to support their findings.

Understanding the Abstract is the first step in understanding the paper. Some papers are focused on a specific question. The paper above asks, 'what parts of the prion protein are essential for its function?' When we read it, we should be focused on that question. Other papers are more descriptive and break little new ground; we may read them for information or for recommendations about future directions of study or about good practice.

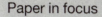

Paper in focus

Pusterla, N., Watson, J.L., Affolter, V.K., Magdesian, K.G., Wilson, W.D. and Carlson, G.P. (2003) 'Purpura haemorrhagica in 53 horses', *Vet. Rec.* 153: 118–21.

The medical records of 53 horses with purpura haemorrhagica were reviewed. Seventeen of them had been exposed to or infected with *Streptococcus equi* [and smaller numbers had been exposed to other pathogens]. The horses were between six months and 19 years of age . . .. The predominant clinical signs were well demarcated subcutaneous oedema of all four limbs and haemorrhages on the visible mucous membranes [and others] . . .. Haematological and biochemical abnormalities [were] commonly detected . . .. All of the horses were treated with corticosteroids . . .. Forty-nine of the horses survived, one died and three were euthanased . . .

It is clear from the Abstract that this paper does not seek to break any very specific new ground or to challenge an orthodox viewpoint. Instead, it reviews existing knowledge, perhaps with a view to drawing conclusions about the aetiology or management of the disease. The Introduction, too, suggests that we should expect a summary of case histories rather than novel findings:

The incidence of purpura haemorrhagica is generally low and sporadic and, although it is well described in many standard textbooks, very few case series have been reported in the literature. This paper describes the history, clinical signs, laboratory values, histopathological findings and outcomes in 53 horses with purpura haemorrhagica.

A clear idea of what kind of paper we are dealing with and what we should expect from it is essential for effective reading. The authors of the paper about horses make a recommendation at the very end concerning the safety of a certain vaccine. However, their recommendation comes from the review of a small sample of horses rather than a systematic trial, and so they quite rightly do not draw attention to the investigation of vaccine safety as a major research goal.

What was the point of the research?

While the Abstract should give you a brief summary of the paper's main findings, the Introduction should situate the research in its

context. Introductions provide a background to the paper and a rationale for the investigation in more detail than is possible in Abstracts.
Here are three of the reasons why it is a good idea to read Introductions
with some care before embarking on the rest of the paper:

- They give you some idea what background information you
  need before starting. If you are not familiar with the background,
  you have an opportunity to find out more about it before reading the
  paper.
- They give you an insight into the authors' starting point and
  approach to the subject.
- They help focus attention on whether the results presented
  in the paper actually address the question they are supposed to
  answer.

Paper in focus

Skerratt, L.F., Skerratt, J.H.L., Banks, S., Martin, R. and Handasyde, K.
(2004) 'Aspects of the ecology of common wombats (*Vombatus ursinus*)
at high density on pastoral land in Victoria', *Aus. J. Zool.* 52: 303–30.

Introduction

Preliminary evidence suggests that the ecology of common wombats
at high densities in agricultural land differs from that of wombats at
lower densities predominantly confined to forest (McIlroy 1973;
Taylor 1993; Buchan and Goldney 1998). Common wombat populations in agricultural landscapes have a much higher food availability in
relation to forest populations . . .. It is also possible that the extent of
burrow sharing among common wombats in high-density populations
differs from that in low-density populations in forest landscapes since
the ratio of burrows to wombats decreases with increasing wombat
density (McIlroy 1973) . . .

Since common wombats are restricted to south-eastern Australia,
where the landscape is predominantly used for agriculture, it is important to understand the ecology of common wombats in agricultural
areas . . .

The Abstract of this paper is a dense summary of research findings
which assumes an understanding of the subject. The Introduction
quoted above gives some pointers towards that understanding. It
stresses the importance of agricultural land as a habitat for wombats,
and the consequent importance of studying the animals' ecology in
agricultural areas as well as in forests. It suggests some questions that
this paper will investigate – for example, the possibility that burrow-
sharing behaviour differs in the two types of habitat. In case you do

not know the background to the subject, the Introduction provides references to earlier work.

When you read the Results section of the paper, you are therefore in a position to evaluate it. You will be familiar with the topic, having followed up appropriate references. You will know what the authors set out to investigate. And you will be able to judge whether the study has made an impact on the understanding of wombat ecology on agricultural land in particular.

☞ **The Abstract and Introduction help you decide whether, why and how to read**

The Abstract and Introduction of MacHine's tastie root paper clearly suffer from major flaws. The overall problem is that the paper makes very striking claims but describes no hard evidence to support them. The evidence that is presented looks like the start of an interesting project about chemicals in food, but the conclusions about health risks go far beyond what is justified. There is a careless muddle about cancer death rates versus cancer incidence. If this were a real paper, I would be inclined to approach it very cautiously indeed.

What are Abstracts *not* for?

Once you have read the Abstract and Introduction, it is tempting to feel like an expert on the paper. After all, the rationale for the work has been explained and a summary of the results has been presented. Why go to the trouble of poring over the whole paper when the important points are right in front of you?

The fact is that this feeling of expertise is illusory. Although introductory sections contain a lot of information, what they omit is crucial. How were the experiments done? Do the raw data really support the conclusions? Are there some confusing findings that do not appear in the Abstract? Are we really getting the full story? The only way to discover the answers is to read the paper properly; the highlights chosen by the authors are no substitute. Once we decide that a paper is worth reading, we should go ahead and read it. If we do not have time, or if a paper is beyond the scope of what we need to know, then that is fine; but having made the decision to stop after the Introduction, we should not deceive ourselves into believing we fully understand what the paper is really about.

Summary

- The Abstract and Introduction should explain why the paper was written.
- They do not give detailed information, but should help you decide how much time to spend on the paper.
- Introductory sections are an entry into a paper – never a substitute for reading it properly.

Professor Stickler sighed again as she picked up her red pen. What was MacHine trying to say? Was this a chemical analysis of tastie roots or a public health study? What sorts of research methods had been used? How did the experimental results relate to the supposed conclusions? This one would need a lot of work before it was ready to publish.

EXERCISE

The following Abstracts are from real papers. For each Abstract

1 explain in no more than two sentences what the paper is about, as far as you can tell from the quoted extract;
2 suggest a title for the paper;
3 make a note of any points that are not clear, or that you would wish to see discussed in more detail later in the paper.

1. Pheromone trails laid by foraging ants serve as a positive feedback mechanism for the sharing of information about food sources. This feedback is nonlinear, in that ants do not react in a proportionate manner to the amount of pheromone deposited. Instead, strong trails elicit disproportionately stronger responses than weak trails. Such nonlinearity has important implications for how a colony distributes its workforce, when confronted with a choice of food sources. We investigated how colonies of the Pharaoh's ant, *Monomorium pharaonis*, distribute their workforce when offered a choice of two food sources of differing energetic value. By developing a nonlinear differential equation model of trail foraging, and comparing model with experiments, we examined how the ants allocate their workforce between the two food sources. In this allocation, the most profitable feeder (i.e. the feeder with the highest concentration of sugar syrup) was usually exploited by the majority of ants. The particular form of the nonlinear feedback in trail foraging means that when we offered the ants a choice between two feeders of equal profitability, foraging was biased to the feeder with the highest initial number of visitors. Taken together, our experiments illuminate how pheromones provide a mechanism whereby ants can efficiently allocate their workforce among the available food sources without centralized control.

2. Lamivudine [β-L-(—)-2′,3′-dideoxy-3′-thiacytidine] is a potent inhibitor of hepadnavirus replication and is used both to treat chronic hepatitis B virus (HBV) infections and to prevent reinfection of transplanted livers. Unfortunately, lamivudine-resistant HBV variants do arise during prolonged therapy, indicating a need for additional antiviral drugs. Replication-competent HBV constructs containing the reverse transcriptase domain L180M/M204V and M204I (rtL180M/M204V and rtM204I) mutations associated with lamivudine resistance were used to produce stable cell lines that express the resistant virus. These cell lines contain stable integrations of HBV sequences and produce both intracellular and extracellular virus. HBV produced by these cell lines was shown to have a marked decrease in sensitivity to lamivudine, with 450- and 3000-fold shifts in the 50% inhibitory concentrations for the rtM204I and rtL180M/M204V viruses, respectively, compared to that for the wild-type virus. Drug assays indicated that the lamivudine-resistant virus exhibited reduced sensitivity to penciclovir [9-(4-hydroxy-3-hydroxymethyl-but-1-yl) guanine] but was still inhibited by the nucleoside analogues CDG (carboxlic 2′-deoxyguanosine) and abacavir {[1S,4R]-4-[2-amino-6-(cyclopropylamino)-9H-purin-9-yl]-2-cyclopentene-1-methanol}. Screening for antiviral compounds active against the lamivudine-resistant HBV can now be done with relative ease.

3. The eye lens is composed of fibre cells, which develop from the epithelial cells on the anterior surface of the lens[1-3]. Differentiation into a lens fibre cell is accompanied by changes in cell shape, the expression of crystallins[4] and the degradation of cellular organelles[5,6]. The loss of organelles is believed to ensure the transparencey of the lens, but the molecular mechanism behind this process is not known. Here we show that DLAD ('DNase II-like acid DNase', also called DNase IIβ) is expressed in human and murine lens cells, and that mice deficient in the DLAD gene are incapable of degrading DNA during lens cell differentiation – the undigested DNA accumulates in the fibre cells. The DLAD−/− mice develop cataracts of the nucleus lentis, and their response to light on electroretinograms is severely reduced. These results indicate that DLAD is responsible for the degradation of nuclear DNA during lens cell differentiation, and that if DNA is left undigested in the lens, it causes cataracts of the nucleus lentis, blocking the light path.

4. Hearts from AC8TG mice develop a higher contractility (LVSP) and larger Ca^{2+} transients than NTG mice, with (surprisingly) no modification in L-type Ca^{2+} channel current ($I_{Ca,L}$) (1). In this study, we examined the cardiac response of AC8TG mice to β-adrenergic and muscarinic agonists and IBMX, a cyclic nucleotide phosphodiesterase (PDE) inhibitor. Stimulation of LVSP and $I_{Ca,L}$ by isoprenaline (ISO, 100 nM) was twofold smaller in AC8TG vs. NTG mice. In contrast, IBMX (100 μM) produced a twofold higher stimulation of $I_{Ca,L}$ in AC8TG vs. NTG mice. IBMX (10 μM) increased LVSP by 40% in both types of mice, but contraction

and relaxation were hastened in AC8TG mice only. Carbachol (10 μM) had no effect on basal contractility in NTG hearts but decreased LVSP by 50% in AC8TG mice. PDE assays demonstrated an increase in cAMP-PDE activity in AC8TG hearts, mainly due to an increase in the hydrolytic activity of PDE4 and PDE1 toward cAMP and a decrease in the activity of PDE1 and PDE2 toward cGMP. We conclude that cardiac expression of AC8 is accompanied by a rearrangement of PDE isoforms, leading to a strong compartmentation of the cAMP signal that shields L-type Ca^{2+} channels and protcts the cardiomyocytes from Ca^{2+} overload.

5. The effects of certain polyphenolic compounds in red wine, such as resveratrol and quercetin, have been widely investigated to determine the relationship between dietary phenolic compounds and the decreased risk of cardiovascular diseases. However, the effects of polyphenolic compounds contained in other foods, such as olive oil, have received less attention and little information exists regarding the biological activities of the phenol fraction in olive oil. The aim of this study was to evaluate the antiplatelet activity and antioxidant power of two isochromans [1-(3′-methoxy-4′-hydroxy-phenyl)-6,7-dihydroxy-isochroman (encoded L116) and 1-phenyl-6,7-dihydroxy-isochroman (encoded L137)] recently discovered in olive oil and synthesized in our laboratory from hydroxytyrosol. These compounds were effective free radical scavengers and inhibited platelet aggregation and thromboxane release evoked by agonists that induce reactive oxygen species-mediated platelet activation including sodium arachidonate and collagen, but not ADP. Release of tritiated arachidonic acid from platelets was also impaired by L116 and L137. These results indicate that other Mediterranean diet nutraceuticals also exhibit antioxidant activity that could be beneficial in the prevention of vascular diseases.

6. The solution structure of the demetalated copper, zinc superoxide dismutase is obtained for the monomeric Glu133Gln/Phe50Glu/Gly51Glu mutant through NMR spectroscopy. The demetalated protein still has a well-defined tertiary structure; however, two β-strands containing two copper ligands (His46 and His48, β4) and one zinc ligand (Asp83, β5) are shortened, and the sheet formed by thse strands and strands β7 and β8 moves away from the other strands of the β-barrel to form an open clam with respect to a closed conformation in the holoprotein. Furthermore, loop IV which contains three zinc ligands (His63, His71 and His80) and loop VII which contributes to the definition of the active cavity channel are severely disordered, and experience extensive mobility as it results from thorough ^{15}N relaxation measurements. These structural and mobility data, if compared with those of the copper-depleted protein and holoprotein, point out the role of each metal ion in the protein folding, leading to the final tertiary structure of the holoprotein, and provide hints for the mechanisms of metal delivery by metal chaperones.

References to these six papers can be found in the Appendix on page 126.

5

Materials and Methods

Materials and Methods

Radichips were purchased from the University canteen. Tests were performed on the following flavours: Jalapeño & Coriander, BBQ Crab & Mustard, and Ready Salted.

Equipment was from LabUltima Supplies unless otherwise specified. Chemical reagents and consumables were from Cheapochem unless otherwise specified.

For each quantitation, 10 g of Radichips were homogenised according to the alkaline extraction method of Slobb *et al.* (1996). Because of other demands on the HPLC equipment, the extracts could not be analysed immediately. Where substantial delays were predicted, extracts were generally frozen at −20°C.

Extracts were then treated as described by Griddle and Byrne (2002). Briefly, the raw homogenate was extracted on diatomaceous earth and eluted with dichloromethane (Sniffy Solvents, Inc.). Eluted extracts were evaporated to dryness and redissolved in 100 μl methanol before HPLC separation. Radicullin was quantitated by u/v fluorescence.

Radicullin extraction and quantitation were performed three times for each flavour, using a fresh bag of Radichips each time.

Professor Stickler's eyes glazed over. Had the boy ever heard of reproducible experimental conditions? Controls? How MacHine had got the job, she simply did not know. Perhaps she should prepare her talk instead and put the manuscript aside until she got back from the conference. On the other hand, how would she be able to enjoy Bermuda knowing what awaited her on her return? She gritted her teeth, gripped the red pen firmly, and soldiered on.

THE SCIENTIFIC METHOD

One of the themes of this book is that we cannot comprehend research publications without putting ourselves in the shoes of researchers. Nowhere is this clearer than when reading Methods sections. Without understanding how authors did their experiments, we are in no position to assess, criticise or build on their results.

Attention please

If you want to replicate an experiment, the Methods section is indispensable. Every detail counts, and there is no point trying to guess what someone did when you can find out for sure. Even if you do not want to reproduce an experiment in its entirety, Methods sections can be extremely helpful and save a lot of time. When we read Materials and Methods in detail, it is often not in order to duplicate other people's work but in order to find stimulating ideas and make connections between different areas. Having a feel for the repertoire of available methods saves us having to devise completely novel ways of doing things. Knowing what materials are available – cell lines, chemicals, pieces of equipment – means that we may not have to reconstruct materials that others have spent time making. If we do not want to duplicate work that has already been done, at least we might be interested in doing something similar or in adapting methodological approaches to our own experiments.

In these circumstances, the value of understanding methods is plain, but most of us frequently read papers whose methodology is not directly relevant to our own work. If we wish neither to replicate nor to adapt the work, need we take the trouble to understand exactly how the results were discovered? The methods used can be quite obscure, and reading them requires concentration and imagination. It is tempting to ignore the methodological parts of a paper and move straight to the 'interesting' part, the Results section. Journals sometimes encourage this by relegating Methods sections to a couple of paragraphs in tiny print at the end of the paper, or by leaving them out completely and making them available only online. It is worth taking a moment to ponder why people bother to publish their methods at all.

If there is one thing that distinguishes science from non-science, it is methodology. In order to be considered scientific, an investigation must adhere to certain principles. There has to be a logical reason why the method can or may answer the question. Defined and reproducible protocols must be followed. Controls must be in place in order to rule out extraneous influences on the results. A detailed Methods section is not just a conventional but essentially arbitrary frill like the umbrella in a piña colada. Rather, it constitutes the evidence that you are reading a scientific paper and not a work of science fiction.

Even if you have no intention of performing an experiment yourself, you still need to know how it was done in order to understand what it means. This is where an empathy with the researcher is so essential. If we have an understanding of how science works, we can ask, 'How would *I* go about answering that question? Does their method do the job? If the method is not scientifically ideal, why not? Is there a good excuse (e.g. an ideal method would involve unethical experiments or use a technology that doesn't exist) or not (e.g. they failed to spot something or slanted the method to get the result they wanted)?'

Tempting as it may be to hurry through dense descriptions of obscure procedures, it is a mistake to do so if the experimental results are important to us. Methodology is at the very heart of science. The results of an experiment, however interesting and exciting, are unscientific if they were not obtained in an appropriate way.

☞ **You cannot judge results without judging methods**

What do you think of Gene MacHine's methods? Are they properly explained? Are they used consistently to produce fair and reliable results? Has sample preparation been standardised in order to take account of differences between flavours, variation between batches of chips, or storage time and conditions since manufacture?

Method or madness?

Imperfect methods do not always spoil the results completely. Sometimes a fraction of the results and conclusions are reliable. Perhaps a method is the best available in the real world, and the results, though uncertain, are the clearest that can be achieved.

🔍 **Paper in focus**

Sneddon, L.U. (2003) 'The evidence for pain in fish: the use of morphine as an analgesic', *Appl. Anim. Behav. Sci.* 83: 153–62.

Before treatment the behaviour and opercular (gill) beat rate were recorded continuously for 15 min. Behaviours measured were use of cover and frequency of swimming activity . . .. Fish were then individually anaesthetised . . . and were carefully injected with the appropriate substance [e.g. 0.1% acetic acid] into the upper and lower frontal lip or handled but not injected . . .. The fish were placed back into their original tank allowing 30 min to recover from the anaesthesia and handling. After this 30 min period, behaviour and opercular beat rate were recorded for 15 min and then the light switched on and food

introduced to the tank. If the fish did not feed they were left for a
further 30 min, then another 15 min of observations were recorded . . ..
This regime continued until the fish actually ingested food.

The above is part of a method to discover whether fish feel pain. Clearly, this
is a very difficult question to answer. If an animal avoids a stimulus, that could
be a purely reflex action; we cannot know that the animal is having a subjective experience of suffering. The author qualifies her choice of method by
explaining the rationale behind it in the paper's Introduction:

The commonly used definition of pain has been proposed by
Zimmerman (1986) and states that pain in animals is an adverse sensory
experience that is caused by a stimulus that can or potentially could
cause tissue damage; this experience should elicit protective motor
(move away from stimulus) and vegetative reactions (e.g. inflammation
and cardiovascular responses) and should also have an adverse
effect on the animal's general behaviour (e.g. cessation of normal
behaviours). So being more than a sensory experience, pain has to be
associated with a 'feeling' or negative perception (Broom, 2000).

This discussion of method is all-important. Authors must define precisely what they are measuring. It is then entirely up to us as readers to
decide how the measurements should be interpreted. We can make this
decision only if we know what the scientists did.

Researchers do not always explain their choice of methods in depth.
Sometimes protocols are presented without much discussion as to
their merits, or the author's thoughts about the limitations of the
method are buried in intricate discussion. This can happen for a variety
of reasons. Authors may wish to present a more black-and-white view
of their experiments than is really warranted. They may fail to notice
problems with their methods. Or they may simply be under pressure
from journals to shorten their manuscripts.

Paper in focus

It is well known that smoking tobacco is a major cause of illness and death.
Tens of papers have also shown that exposure to other people's tobacco
smoke ('passive smoking' or 'secondary smoking') increases the risk of dying
from diseases such as lung cancer and heart disease. The International
Agency for Research on Cancer (part of the World Health Organisation) concluded after a large international review of published work that 'second-hand
tobacco smoke IS carcinogenic to humans' (Press release 141, June 2002).

Enstrom, J.E. and Kabat, G.C. (2003) 'Environmental tobacco smoke
and tobacco related mortality in a prospective study of Californians,
1960–98', BMJ 326: 1057–66.

> Exposure to environmental tobacco smoke was not significantly associated with the death rate for coronary heart disease, lung cancer, or chronic obstructive pulmonary disease in men or women.

Contradicting as it does such a widely accepted view, the result presented here is certainly striking: the journal responded with a front cover splash, a brief highlight in the section *This week in the BMJ* and an editorial. The story was widely reported in the media, inevitably without methodological details. How then was exposure to second-hand smoke measured?

> Exposure to environmental tobacco smoke [was] based on smoking status of the spouse in 1959, 1965, and 1972. Never smokers married to current or former smokers were compared with never smokers married to never smokers . . . .. The smoking status of spouses as of 1959 was related to three self reported measures of exposure to environmental tobacco smoke as of 1999.

The measure of secondary smoke exposure for 1960–98 turns out to be whether a person's spouse smoked between 1959 and 1972. The small proportion of subjects still alive in 1999 were also asked to describe whether they had ever regularly been exposed to cigarette smoke from others in work or daily life. However, by this time they were largely elderly and were being asked to summarise their exposure decades earlier in a simple descriptor.

Second-hand smoke was so pervasive in the 1950s that many people could easily have had some exposure even if their spouse did not smoke. In this paper, many people described themselves as having been regularly exposed to smoke in work or daily life even though their spouse was a non-smoker. People who spent their entire working lives in smoke-filled workplaces but were married to non-smokers were classified in this study as not exposed. If they died from lung cancer or heart disease, the study would not attribute this to the effects of secondary smoke.

In addition, spousal smoking status was determined only up to 1972, except for the small proportion of subjects who survived to 1999 and responded to the questionnaire. People whose spouses gave up smoking between 1973 and 1999 were still classified as exposed. If they managed to survive that period, the study would regard that as an endorsement for the safety of secondary smoke. Both of these misclassifications dilute the contrast between the 'exposed' and the 'unexposed' groups.

Like the experiment on pain in fish, this research also tackles a very difficult area. The only direct way to measure environmental tobacco smoke exposure would be to fit people with a mask at birth and record everything that enters their lungs over the course of their lifetime, clearly an absurd proposition. All researchers in this field (and many other fields) are forced to use imperfect methods. Likewise, all careful readers have to weigh up the evidence presented and to decide what conclusions they can realistically draw. Many people wrote to the *British Medical Journal* about this paper. Some of them thought the scientific problems were so grave that they invalidated the results entirely, while others defended the results despite the difficulties with classifying smoke exposure accurately.

☞ Imperfect methods are a fact of life – it is up to the reader to judge them

Although good methods are the gold standard of science, they do not always have the brightest gleam. Unscientific or unsuitable methods can look very attractive. So how do we recognise experiments that are sound and dependable?

Ideally, a scientific method should be

* direct
* robust.

A *direct* method is one that tells us directly what we want to know. A direct method for estimating the density of bacteria in a culture would be to take a sample and count the bacteria. An *indirect* method is one that generates an observation from which we can infer what we want to know. An indirect way to estimate the density of bacteria in a culture would be to measure the optical density of the culture – essentially how cloudy it is – and use that to calculate the density of cells.

You may wonder what is wrong with indirect methods, especially if you are familiar with measuring the cell density of bacterial cultures, which is invariably done through optical density (OD) measurements. The answer is that in an indirect method, there is a deductive or inferential step between the observation and the conclusion. All deductions and inferences rely on making assumptions, and assumptions are liable to be wrong. The more assumptions must be made in converting an observation into a conclusion, the more room there is for error. To return to our bacterial culture example, in the direct counting method, the only assumptions we make are (i) that the sample we took was representative of the whole culture and (ii) that we counted correctly. In the OD method, we similarly assume that the sample was representative and that we measured OD correctly. However, we also assume that the conversion from OD readings to cell density works reliably. Because this assumption has been tested many times and has been found safe, we routinely rely on it since in this case the indirect method is much more convenient than trying to count individual bacteria. But when we read papers we need to notice how indirect a method is and what assumptions have been made before deciding how much to trust the results.

Paper in focus

Gorre, M.E., Mohammed, M., Ellwood, K., Hsu, N., Paquette, R., Rao, P.N. and Sawyers, C.L. (2001) 'Clinical resistance to STI–571 cancer therapy caused by BCR-ABL gene mutation or amplification', *Science* 293: 876–80.

The most direct measure of signaling through the BCR-ABL pathway is through the enzymatic activity of BCR-ABL protein itself [BCR-ABL is a kinase] . . . . Although readily measured in cell lines, this assay is difficult to perform in a reproducible, quantitative fashion with clinical material because BCR-ABL is subject to rapid degradation . . . upon cell lysis (15). In a search for alternative measures of BCR-ABL kinase activity, we found that the phosphotyrosine content of Crkl, an adaptor protein that is specifically and constitutively phosphorylated by BCR-ABL in CML cells . . . could be measured reproducibly and quantitatively in clinical specimens.

It is not necessary to understand the science behind this extract in order to realise that the researchers ran into a problem. They wished (for reasons that are explained in the paper) to measure the enzymatic activity of a protein called BCR-ABL. However, BCR-ABL is unstable and rapidly becomes degraded in clinical specimens. Therefore they were forced to measure its activity indirectly by looking at another protein. Here is an example of a good excuse being used to justify an indirect method: the method of choice was unusable because the protein is not stable enough. In this case, the authors explained clearly why they could not use a more direct method. It is up to us as readers to decide whether the method used gives a reliable indication of BCR-ABL activity, which is what the investigators really wanted to measure.

☞ Direct experiments require less interpretation than indirect ones

A *robust* method is one that tries to eliminate misinterpretations by approaching a problem from several different angles.

Paper in focus

Zhang, Y., Hoon, M.A., Chandrashekar, J., Mueller, K.L., Cook, B., Wu, D., Zuker, C.S. and Ryba, N.J.P. (2003) 'Coding of sweet, bitter, and umami tastes: different receptor cells sharing similar signaling pathways', *Cell* 112: 293–301.

> To define the role of [the taste receptor protein] TRPM5 in taste, we generated knockout mice that lack a functional TRPM5 protein . . ... Figure 3 shows antibody labeling experiments demonstrating a complete lack of TRPM5 staining in homozygous KO [knockout] animals. In order to ensure that loss of TRPM5 did not affect the viability or integrity of taste cells, we also compared the expression of [other taste receptors] in control and KO animals; no significant differences were observed . . .
>
> To examine the taste responses of the genetically modified mice, we recorded tastant-induced action potentials from the two major nerves innervating taste receptor cells of the tongue . . ... In control mice, a variety of sweet, amino acid, bitter, sour, and salty stimuli elicit robust nerve responses (Figure 4). In contrast, responses to sweet, amino acid, and bitter stimuli are essentially abolished in the knockout animals (Figure 4). Indeed, we tested a panel of 9 sweet, 10 amino acid, and 6 bitter tastants, and in all cases failed to elicit a significant response. Notably, TRPM5 KO animals retain normal responses to salty or sour stimuli. A strong prediction of these physiological results is that TRPM5 KO mice should have severely compromised behavioral responses to sweet, bitter, and amino acid tastants, but normal salty and sour taste. Therefore, we examined taste behavior by measuring taste choices in two-bottle intake preference assays or by directly counting immediate licking responses in a 16-stimulus channel gustometer (see Experimental Procedures) . . . [T]he ability of the KO animals to taste sweet, bitter, or amino acid stimuli is completely abolished. However, both the KO and wild-type animals were equally sensitive to salty or sour stimuli.

The authors used a molecular-biological method (not described in this excerpt) to knock out the Trpm5 gene. The method should reveal unambiguously whether the gene has been knocked out. However, to be doubly sure, the researchers confirmed that the knockout has succeeded by trying and failing to detect the TRPM5 protein that the gene produces.

☞ Results should be confirmed with independent experiments

They then measured the taste sensitivity of the knockout animals using two different methods: (i) direct measurement of nerve stimulation and (ii) behavioural response to tastants like sugars, amino acids and so on. What was the point of doing both experiments? Surely if sweet, bitter and amino acid tastants failed to elicit nerve excitation, it was obvious that the animals would not have a behavioural response to those substances because they could not taste them.

Strictly speaking, it *is* obvious. But there is more to it than that.

What about the positive nerve response of the knockout mice to salt and sour stimuli? Does that nerve excitation cause a subjective sensation of taste, so that the mice would respond behaviourally? Only a behaviour test will tell. Conversely, the behaviour test on its own would have been indirect. If knockout mice do not find sugar solution attractive, we can deduce that it is probably because they cannot taste it; but we cannot know for sure. The nerve excitation measurement tells us directly that the sense of taste is defective. Finally, doing a double experiment is a safeguard against mistakes. It is unlikely, but just possible, that the nerve stimulation results were artefacts, perhaps resulting from faulty measurement, mixing up tastants, or the difficulty of recording tiny electrical pulses in the nerves of anaesthetised mice. Similarly, it is conceivable that the behaviour test results were artefacts resulting from the small samples used (four mice each tested twice) or from the difficulty of observing and measuring their rate of licking from water bottles. Implausible though these scenarios are, they cannot be ruled out. However, since the two sets of experiments agree perfectly, it would be perverse to suggest that they both just happened to be incorrect in exactly the same way.

 Results are more reliable the more lines of evidence support them

What are controls for?

If I give a drug to twenty people with headaches and fifteen of them are completely better within an hour, that proves the drug must be pretty effective. Or does it? How do I know the patients would not have recovered just as quickly on their own? How can I prove it? Obviously it is impossible to go back in time and try out what happens if I do not administer the drug; so what should I do instead?

One of the hallmarks of a good method is the choice of suitable controls. In the case of drug trials such as the one described above, normal practice is to use two groups of patients. Patients in one group get the drug, while those in the other group get a placebo. The crucial point is that there should be no relevant differences between the patients in the two groups other than the treatment they receive. Giving the drug to all the women and a placebo to all the men would not be a sensible idea: we do not know that men and women have similar kinds of headache, nor that they respond similarly to the test drug, so any differences we find between the groups may be due to the sex of the subjects rather than the choice of treatment.

More generally, since we cannot go back in time and repeat experiments under two sets of conditions, the idea is to run parallel experiments that differ *only in the one respect that we are interested in*. All other variables should be controlled, in other words held constant between the two test runs. Actually, to do this perfectly is impossible: the two runs will not occupy identical portions of the laboratory bench or the test site; they may not take place at identical times; we may not be wearing the same clothes on both occasions.

☞ Uncontrolled variables can confound results

   This is where the fun begins. It is the scientist's responsibility to make an educated guess about which factors may make a difference to an experiment (and therefore need controlling) and which factors are irrelevant. If you are doing an experiment on wild bird populations, it matters hugely whether it is summer or winter, but not whether it is Monday or Tuesday. If you are growing bacteria in a temperature-controlled warm room, the season should not matter but the number of hours or days since you last changed the growth medium certainly will. It is the reader's responsibility to evaluate the controls and to decide how adequate they are.

Paper in focus

Ramenofsky, M.L. and Leape, L.L. (1981) 'Continuous upper esophageal pH monitoring in infants and children with gastroesophageal reflux, pneumonia, and apneic spells', *J. Pediatr. Surg.* 16: 374–8.

Reflux of stomach contents into the oesophagus can cause heartburn in adults. In infants, reflux that reaches the upper oesophagus has been implicated as a factor in recurrent pneumonia and apnea (temporary cessation of breathing). This article investigates whether severe reflux can be lessened by feeding a thickened formula and/or by placing babies in particular positions before and after feeding. Various combinations of formula and position are used over a 24-hour period, during which babies are monitored continuously for reflux.

   The infant was positioned initially in a chalasia chair [an adjustable infant seat] at 60° for 4 hr, then supine [on its back] for 4 hr and finally, prone [on its front] for 4 hr (Fig. 2). Unthickened feedings of standard infant formula were given on hours 2, 6 and 10. The volume of feedings was appropriate for the child's weight. During the second 12 hr of the test the same positioning and feeding sequences were used, but feedings were thickened with 1 tablespoon of rice cereal per ounce of formula. Results were analysed by 2-hr periods, before feeding . . . and after feeding . . .. Twelve 2-hr study periods were available for evaluation [i.e. the two hours before and after each feed, with six feeds in various combinations of formula and position].

The researchers have surmised that position and feed thickness might have an effect on reflux, and the various two-hour study periods differ in respect of the baby's position and feed formula. Are these two variables the *only* differences between the study periods? Clearly not. The experiment ran for a full 24 hours. If the monitoring period for every baby started at the same time of day (we are not told whether this was the case) then perhaps all the unthickened feeds were given during the day and all the thickened feeds at night or *vice versa*. Furthermore, the order of the treatments was the same for all the babies. For example, the supine position always followed a period in the chair and never a period of lying prone.

Do these design features affect the reliability of the test? Perhaps not. Maybe different infants started the monitoring period at different times of day, effectively jumbling formula thickness with respect to the night/day cycle. Maybe the night/day cycle is unimportant anyway. Maybe the position in which a baby was lying two hours ago is not relevant to its reflux now. These questions are not discussed in the paper, and as a non-expert in the field, I cannot tell whether variables like time of day and previous position need controlling or not.

☞ Every relevant variable should be controlled

THE SCIENTIFIC QUESTION

The methodological approach we have discussed is a rigorous way of approaching a defined problem. If we have not formulated the problem clearly enough, it can be very difficult to judge the method or interpret the results.

A clear problem

🔍 **Paper in focus**

English, J.S.C., Bunker, C.B., Ruthven, K., Dowd, P.M. and Greaves, M.W. (1989) 'A double-blind comparison of the efficacy of betamethasone dipropionate cream twice daily versus once daily in the treatment of steroid responsive dermatoses', *Clin. Exp. Dermatol.* 14: 32–4.

Topical steroids have been grouped into four categories depending upon their rank order of potency . . .. The side-effects of topical corticosteroids . . . increase with the potency of the steroids used, yet the optimum frequency of application has not been satisfactorily established . . .. The aim of this study has been to determine whether a potent topical steroid is as effective applied once as opposed to twice daily in the treatment of eczema and psoriasis.

This was a double-blind comparative study of 3 weeks duration. Patients with endogenous eczema (atopic, hand or discoid) or chronic plaque psoriasis were allocated randomly to either twice daily (b.d.) treatment with betamethasone dipropionate cream (0.05%) or daily (o.d.), with betamethasone dipropionate cream (0.05%) in the morning and base cream in the evening . . .

Patients were analysed according to disease category; either eczema or psoriasis . . .

Thirty-eight patients had atopic eczema, 19 hand eczema and six discoid eczema. There was no significant difference in distribution of the types of eczema between the o.d. and b.d. groups. There were 33 patients in the o.d. group; their ages ranged from 20 to 74 years . . .. In the b.d. group there were 32 patients whose ages ranged from 18 to 67 years . . .. Fifty patients completed 3 weeks treatment [and the other 15 either stopped because their condition had improved, or were withdrawn for various reasons] . . .

There were no significant differences between those patients in the once daily and twice daily treatment regimes for all the symptoms and signs after 3 weeks treatment.

This study aimed to compare the efficacy of two treatment regimes for eczema and psoriasis. However, the term 'eczema' refers to a number of distinct conditions; yet the patients were analysed as a group, with no separate presentation of results for the different conditions. The authors do not state or demonstrate that patients with different types of eczema, ranging in age from 18 to 74, respond in the same way to betamethasone, either in terms of how effective the treatment is or in terms of the side-effect profile. Without evidence to the contrary, we must consider the possibility that different conditions respond differently.

This is an example of a method that may not be sufficiently well defined to give meaningful results. It is also worth noting how small the samples were, particularly if we treat the different types of eczema separately. In the following chapter, we shall see that it is very difficult to demonstrate a significant difference between small samples. The lack of difference seen here could be connected with the size of the samples.

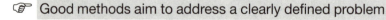 Good methods aim to address a clearly defined problem

Summary

- The choice of methods is at the heart of all scientific research.
- Methods are frequently imperfect for a variety of reasons.
- Readers should regard direct, robust methods with good controls as the ideal.
- It is difficult to interpret results from an uncertain question.
- Readers should look for methods that ask clear questions about well-defined situations.

EXERCISE

The following extracts are from real papers. For each extract, comment on the methodology used. For each extract

1 try to work out the purpose of the method described;
2 comment on its strengths;
3 comment on any weaknesses or limitations, as far as you can tell from the quoted extract;
4 suggest any points that you would expect to see discussed in the rest of the paper.

1. The concentration of total Polη [an enzyme involved in DNA replication] was determined using two methods. First, the UV absorbance at 280 nM was measured under denaturing conditions (8 M urea) using a molar extinction coefficient equal to 78,896 M^{-1}cm^{-1} (calculated from the amino acid composition). Second, the Bio-Rad Protein Assay was used with bovine serum albumin as a standard. Both methods gave similar results. In addition, the concentration of active Polη was determined by active-site titration (see Results; Figure 2). Comparing the concentration of total Polη to the concentration of active Polη, we found that the preparation of Polη used in this study was 80% active. The concentration of Polη used in all experiments was corrected for the amount of active Polη.

   From Washington, M.T., Prakash, L. and Prakash, S. (2001) 'Yeast DNA polymerase η utilizes an induced-fit mechanism of nucleotide incorporation', *Cell* 107: 917–27.

2. . . . the introduction of species by man, whether directly or indirectly, to regions far from their centres of origin, is one of the main causes of biodiversity loss . . .

   In particular, it is known that introduced herbivores can cause significant impacts on biological diversity . . .. This has been shown for grassland birds . . .. Among the mechanisms responsible for this impact, it is generally accepted that herbivores can affect the breeding success of birds, both directly by reducing the number of available nesting sites or by nest trampling . . . and indirectly by exposing them to predators . . .

We selected two replicates from each grazing regime to compare egg predation in areas of intensive grazing by feral horses with that in sectors of moderate or no grazing. We placed 10 quail (*Coturnix coturnix japonicus*) eggs, which are similar in size to the eggs of typical Pampas grassland birds (De la Peña, 1987), in each of two 100 m transects in each replicate. We put the eggs directly on the ground underneath the bush or clump of grass closest to the sampling point, in order to mimic the nesting habitat described by De la Peña (1987) and to avoid unconscious bias in their placement. We visited the transects every 3 days over a period of 14 days and recorded the number of broken or missing eggs per transect and we compared the percentage of predation in each habitat using a *t*-test.

From Zalba, S.M. and Cozzani, N.C. (2004) 'The impact of feral horses on grassland bird communities in Argentina', *Anim. Conserv.* 7: 35–44.

3. Two independent methods were used to confirm that WC-2 specifically and directly associates with FRQ. First, bacterially expressed and purified glutathione S-transferase (GST)–WC-2 fusion proteins or GST alone (see Materials and methods) were incubated with *in vitro* translated, ^{35}S-labeled FRQ or, as a negative control, the irrelevant protein luciferase (Figure 3A and B). SDS-PAGE analysis of the bound proteins indicates that FRQ binds to GST–WC-2 but not to GST alone. In contrast, no detectable binding of luciferase to either GST–WC-2 or GST was seen (Figure 3A).

This *in vitro* WC-2–FRQ interaction was confirmed with proteins made *in vivo* (Figure 3B). Lysates from cultures grown 24 h in the dark were subjected to immunoprecipitation with either WC-2 antiserum or pre-immune serum (see Materials and methods). Both FRQ and WC-1 co-immunoprecipitated with WC-2. These proteins were not detected in precipitates of extracts incubated with pre-immune antisera. Similar results were obtained in reciprocal experiments using either the FRQ or WC-1 antisera and checking for WC-2 co-immunoprecipitation (Figure 3C; data not shown).

From Denault, D.L., Loros, J.J. and Dunlap, J.C. (2001) 'WC-2 mediates FRQ–WC-1 interaction within the PAS protein-linked circadian feedback loop of *Neurospora*', *EMBO J.* 20: 109–17.

4. For exchange, the subject was given a token that could immediately be returned to the experimenter for a food reward. The experimenter (S.F.B.) stood before the monkey with the left hand outstretched in a palm-up begging gesture, approximately 5 cm above the floor of the test chamber and 2 cm from the mesh, and with the right hand in the laboratory coat pocket. No other cues were given to encourage the monkey, and no reward was shown before correct exchange. The monkey had 60 s to place the token into the palm of the experimenter's outstretched hand. Throwing the token at the experimenter or out of the test chamber did not count as an exchange. After a successful return, the experimenter lifted the correct reward from a transparent bowl visible to [the exchanger] and gave it to the exchanger.

From Brosnan, S.F. and de Waal, F.B.M. (2003) 'Monkeys reject unequal pay', *Nature* 425: 297–9.

5. Homeostatically dividing T cells [cells dividing to reconstitute the immune system after T cell loss] can eventually acquire functional features of pathogenic T cells after multiple rounds of replication . . .. We asked whether the proliferating T cell population in NOD [non obese diabetic] mice could become tissue destructive [attacking islet cells in the pancreas and ultimately causing diabetes]. Interestingly, the rapidly proliferating CD44+ T cells . . . induced lysis of purified islet cells from NOD mice (Figure 4B) but did not lyse control [immunologically mismatched] islet cells (data not shown). In contrast, quiescent T cells did not induce lysis of islet cells from either strain (Figure 4B and data not shown). More importantly, the actively proliferating . . . T cell population rapidly induced diabetes in vivo (Figure 4C). Clearly, the T cells undergoing rapid turnover demonstrated specific self-tissue-destructive capability.

From King, C., Ilic, A., Koelsch, K. and Sarvetnick, N. (2004) 'Homeostatic expansion of T cells during immune insufficiency generates autoimmunity', *Cell* 117: 265–77.

6. Reflexology . . . is based on the theory that all organs are represented by various points on the feet, forming a map of the whole body, and that massaging specific areas of feet can affect corresponding target organs . . .

Our clinical experience indicated that paresthesias [abnormal sensations in the skin] and spasticity [susceptibility to muscle spasms] in MS [multiple sclerosis] and in patients with other disorders could be alleviated by reflexology . . .

Patients were randomized . . .. Each reflexologist treated one study and one control patient. Patients in the study group received full reflexology treatment which included manual pressure on specific points of foot soles and massage of the calf area, while patients in the control group received sham treatment of nonspecific massage of the calf, providing control for touch therapy and general relaxation. The patients in both groups were therefore exposed to the same therapists. All patients received equal number and duration of treatment sessions . . .

Patients were informed that they are going to receive reflexology treatment targeted mainly either to the sole (study) or to the calf area (controls), while the efficacy of each is yet to be determined. The reflexologists were instructed not to discuss the efficacy of either treatment with the patients . . .

Critics of complementary therapies often present the argument that placebo effects comprise most of their therapeutic effect, partly due to patient's expectations, the compassion of the therapist and to the relaxing atmosphere of private clinics[16]. In order to overcome this obstacle, we performed all treatments in the facility of a hospital clinic. A design of control treatment has been also given a careful consideration. We considered the difficulty presented to reflexologists to avoid touching specific points of the feet. Therefore, a nonspecific massage of the calf (rather than of the feet area) was chosen as sham therapy . . .

From Siev-Ner, I., Gamus, D., Lerner-Geva, L. and Achiron, A. (2003) 'Reflexology treatment relieves symptoms of multiple sclerosis: a randomized controlled study', *Multiple Sclerosis* 9: 356–61.

7. Over one third of US smokers attempt cessation each year[1-5]; however, the success rate per attempt is low .... During the 1990s, following clinical trials indicating efficacy, a variety of pharmaceutical cessation aids became available .... In the controlled-trial setting, with well-monitored protocols, nicotine replacement therapy (NRT) and the anti-depressant bupropion increased success for moderate to heavy smokers (≥ 15 cigarettes/d) by 50% to 100%.[11-18] There is no consensus of a benefit for light smokers (<15 cigarettes/d).

... Since then, the nicotine patch became available over-the-counter in 1996 ...

In 1999, we examined duration of aid use, if aid users would recommend these products to other smokers, whether assistance in paying for the medication was associated with longer use, and the use of adjuvant behavioral assistance. Finally, we searched for evidence that, collectively, pharmaceutical aids increased successful cessation among moderate to heavy and light smokers.

... Respondents [to a questionnaire] were asked about current smoking status, whether they smoked a year previously and how much, whether they had in the past year quit intentionally for a day or longer, which is the standard definition of a meaningful cessation attempt,[27] how long they were off cigarettes the last time they attempted cessation, and if they used a pharmaceutical aid or had other assistance for their most recent attempt in the last year. If so, they were asked how long they used the aid, whether they would recommend it to a friend, and who paid for it ...

In 1999, although collectively pharmaceutical aids helped moderate to heavy smokers discontinue using cigarettes longer, they were not associated with a clinically meaningful long-term improvement in successful cessation, and no benefit was observed for light smokers. In 1992, NRT was prescribed by physicians only, and physicians or pharmacists may have provided counseling about product use ... [I]n 1999 ... all NRT was obtained over-the-counter ...

This study adds to concerns that the efficacy of pharmaceutical aids observed in clinical trials may not extend to effectiveness in the general population ...

From Pierce, J.P. and Gilpin, E.A. (2002) 'Impact of over-the-counter sales on effectiveness of pharmaceutical aids for smoking cessation', *JAMA* 288: 1260–4.

8. To corroborate the role of [the protein] versican V1 in neuronal differentiation, rat neural stem cells were isolated and cocultured with rat astroglial cells that had been transiently transfected with versican V1 construct or a control vector. V1 expression was confirmed by Western blot (our unpublished data). The neural stem cells in both neurospheres [small clumps of cells that form after a few days in culture] and individual cells were seeded on the top of the astroglial cells and incubated for 6 d. The neurospheres cocultured with V1-transfected astroglial cells exhibited increased numbers of processes compared with these cocul-

tured with vector-transfected cells (Figure 2, A and B). Stained with anti-MAP-2ab antibody for neuronal differentiation (Song *et al.*, 2002), the neurospheres cocultured with V1-transfected astroglial cells exhibited significantly increased positively stained cells than those cocultured with vector-transfected cells (Figure 2C).

From Wu, Y., Sheng, W., Chen, L., Dong, H., Lee, V., Lu, F., Wong, C.S., Lu, W.-Y. and Yang, B.B. (2004) 'Versican V1 isoform induces neuronal differentiation and promotes neurite outgrowth', *Mol. Biol. Cell* 15: 2093–104.

9. A search of the databases identified 49 acetate kinase sequences from diverse prokaryotes with identities to the M. *thermophila* enzyme that range from 37 to 65%. Five arginines in the M. *thermophila* acetate kinase are highly conserved with the homologous sequences . . .. The five conserved arginines in M. *thermophila* were individually replaced with alanine, leucine, or lysine to assess their function . . .

Replacement of R91 and R241 with alanine produced variants with specific activities of approximately $0.5\,\mu$mol min^{-1} (mg of protein)$^{-1}$ that were near the limit of detection and less than 0.1% of recombinant wild-type [740 $\pm$ 80μmol min^{-1} (mg of protein)$^{-1}$] . . .. Additional experiments to verify the structural integrity of the R91A and R241A variants were performed. Gel filtration indicated that the R91A and R241A variants were dimeric in accordance with recombinant wild-type and authentic acetate kinase. The circular dichroism spectra of the R241A variant and recombinant wild-type were superimposable (data not shown) while the spectra of the R91A variant and recombinant wild-type varied only slightly (Figure 2) . . .. These results indicate no global conformational changes occurred in the R91A and R241A variants compared to recombinant wild-type. Thus, the low specific activities of the variants suggested that R91 and R241 are essential for catalysis.

From Singh-Wissmann, K., Miles, R.D., Ingram-Smith, C. and Ferry, J.G. (2000) 'Identification of essential arginines in the acetate kinase from *Methanosarcina thermophila*', *Biochemistry* 39: 3671–7.

10. One hundred ninety-two unrelated patients with affective disorder (94 bipolar type I, 33 bipolar type II, and 65 unipolar) and 142 normal control subjects were personally interviewed with the Structured Clinical Interview for DSM-III-R-Lifetime Version (Spitzer et al 1990), screening DSM-IV criteria (American Psychiatric Association 1994). The sample of affected patients was on average 45.3 years old (SD = 14.4), were predominantly (63.0%) female and were mostly (71.5%) recruited as in-patients. Each patient who had a first-degree relative with a history of mood disorders (or suicidal attempts) was classified as having a positive family history.

The healthy control group was recruited at a recreation center for old people. This control group, aged 60 years or older, did not have any positive personal and/or familial history (elicited through interview of the proband only) of psychiatric disorders. Control subjects were on average 73.6 years old (SD = 8.3), were mostly (54.2%) female, and only 4.9% had a professional activity.

From Bonnier, B., Gorwood, P., Hamon, M., Sarfati, Y., Boni, C. and Hardy-Bayle, M.-C. (2002) 'Association of 5-HT$_{2A}$ receptor gene polymorphism with major affective disorders: the case of a subgroup of bipolar disorder with low suicide risk', *Biol. Psychiat.* 51: 762–5.

6

Quantitative methods

Results

We re-examined the correlation between the consumption of tastie root and the death rate from liver cancer (Lyse, Damlise and Statz, 2001). The correlation coefficient for six European countries (excluding France) is 0.52 (data not shown). The correlation is significantly higher in northern Europe (Belgium, the Netherlands and the UK) than in Mediterranean Europe (Greece, Italy and Spain).

The radicullin concentrations found in various samples of Radichips are shown in table 1. Although the mean concentrations for two flavours are below 0.2 ng/g, the mean for BBQ Crab & Mustard is 0.4 ng/g. This difference may be attributed to our finding of over 0.8 ng/g in one of the bags sampled, about three times higher than in any other bag of any flavour. This finding is of considerable importance. If different samples contain wildly different amounts of radicullin, it is virtually impossible to determine a safe upper limit for Radichip consumption: a few bags of Radichips could contain the whole safe annual dose of radicullin! Since the variance of radicullin concentration is much greater in BBQ Crab & Mustard than in the other flavours tested, we suggest that BBQ Crab & Mustard be withdrawn from sale immediately as a precautionary measure until we have further investigated the cause of this variation.

Beads of perspiration began to glisten on Professor Stickler's brow. Keep calm, she told herself, keep calm and don't hyperventilate. She pressed heavily on the surface of the manuscript. The red pen was beginning to run out.

SIGNIFICANT FIGURES

If we lived in a uniform world, we wouldn't need statistics. Scientists like Gene MacHine would make measurements and present them in the knowledge that they were perfectly reliable and reproducible. If we gave a pill to a person with a headache and the headache got better in an hour, then that would be the exact length of time to recovery for every patient. We would know exactly where we were.

Needless to say, the world is not like that. The measurements that scientists make are subject to variation, for all kinds of reasons. Some variation results from imperfect measurement: it is impossible to measure anything with absolute precision, and the error is likely to differ between measurements. Some variation is due to natural differences between subjects (my headache may take an hour to get better while my friend's takes half an hour) or within subjects (today I may recover in an hour; tomorrow, it might take me two hours).

With such variability affecting scientific measurements, how can we be sure that we are measuring real effects? Just performing a control is not enough. Even if there turns out to be a difference between the experimental and control measurements, how do we tell whether it is due to chance or to a real effect? Natural variability cannot be controlled, so how do we take account of it in analysing the results? The point of statistical analysis is to solve that puzzle and give the best possible estimate of whether results reflect genuine effects or not.

This section is not about particular statistical techniques or how to perform statistical tests. Our purpose is much more limited: to investigate some simple questions that readers should ask of any statistical analysis appearing in research papers. In the next section, we apply similar principles of active reading to pictorial and graphical data.

Statistical significance

One important measure associated with the risk of statistical artefacts is a result's level of 'statistical significance'. A typical result would be a finding of difference between an experimental group and a control group subjected to different treatments. For example, people given vitamin C for a cold might take 4½ days to recover on average, while people given a placebo might take five days on average. The difference could have arisen in two ways: either there is a real difference between treatments, or there is no underlying difference but we saw one in this experiment because of random variation.

Imagine the second scenario, where there is no underlying difference between the samples. What would be the chance that the half-day difference we saw arose through statistical variation? The chance can be calculated, and is reported as a 'P value', which can be defined as the probability that an effect as big as the one observed (or bigger) will arise by chance if there is no underlying difference between groups. A high P value means that the observed result could easily arise by chance even from identical populations. When the P value is very low, the result is said to be statistically significant.

For example, take this extract from Irnich *et al.* (2001): '[t]he reduction in pain related to motion was significantly greater in the acupuncture group compared with the massage group (P = 0.0052).' The result is from a comparison of acupuncture with massage for neck pain relief. Acupuncture was found to be more effective than massage for relieving motion-induced pain; but was acupuncture really superior or did it just get lucky in this particular sample? The phrase 'P = 0.0052' tells us that if acupuncture and massage really had identical effects on pain, there would be only a 0.0052 probability of observing as great a difference as the researchers found (or a greater difference) through chance alone. Since this probability is so small, it makes sense to ascribe the observed superiority of acupuncture to a genuine difference between treatments.

By convention, results are often deemed noteworthy if they have a P value less than or equal to 0.05. When this occurs they are said to be statistically significant at the 5% level. The smaller the value of P, the greater the degree of statistical significance, and the more confident we can be that the difference between treatments really is genuine. The convention of taking 5% as the cutoff is more or less arbitrary, and is certainly not used for every analysis in every paper. Statistical significance is a continuum: a result does not suddenly become 'true' because it is significant at the 5% level. Conversely, a result does not become meaningless if P > 0.05. This is worth bearing in mind: you will sometimes see any result with P ≤ 0.05 described as 'significant' and any result with P > 0.05 described as 'not significant'. Two papers testing the same thing and finding P values of 0.049 and 0.051 could then be described as 'conflicting studies', which is clearly absurd.

It is also vital to remember that statistical significance is purely a technical term in statistics. On its own, it says nothing at all about scientific or clinical interest.

Paper in focus

Rowan, T.G., Sarasola, P., Sunderland, S.J., Giles, C.J. and Smith, D.G. (2004) 'Efficacy of danofloxacin in the treatment of respiratory disease in European cattle', *Vet. Rec.* 154: 585–9.

By day 1 the treatment with danofloxacin had resulted in a rapid reduction to a mean rectal temperature of 38.9°C, significantly lower than the mean rectal temperature of the animals treated with tilmicosin, which was 39.1°C (P < 0.05) . . . there was a significant difference on day 10 [of treatment] (P < 0.05). However, the differences on days 1 and 10 were considered to be of no clinical relevance because the animals' temperature remained within the normal body temperature range.

The reader may wonder why the researchers took the trouble to quote the statistical analysis when the findings are not clinically relevant. Here is an example of the opposite phenomenon:

Blackhall, F.H., Ranson, M., Radford, J.A., Hancock, B.W., Soukop, M., McGown, A.T., Robbins, A., Halbert, G. and Jayson, G.C. (2001) 'A phase II trial of bryostatin 1 in patients with non-Hodgkin's lymphoma', *Brit. J. Cancer* 84: 465–9.

The results fail to demonstrate efficacy of this regimen of bryostatin 1 in the treatment of NHL [non-Hodgkin's lymphoma]. In light of preclinical data that demonstrate synergy between bryostatin 1 and several cytotoxic agents and cytokines, clinical studies to investigate bryostatin 1 in combination are warranted.

In this case, the researchers override the lack of statistically significant results to recommend that further studies be undertaken nonetheless, on the clinical grounds that bryostatin might be more efficacious if combined with other drugs.

The above papers recognise that statistical analysis should always serve scientific or clinical judgement and never supersede it. Readers need to consider whether a result is scientifically interesting before they even bother asking whether it is statistically significant.

☞ Statistical significance is quite distinct from scientific relevance

The way statistical significance is defined means that even if two populations are really identical, we will sometimes see statistically significant differences when we compare samples taken from those populations. The more results we look at, the more likely we are to find one that, despite statistical significance, is actually due to random fluctuation.

It is particularly important to look out for artefactual findings of significance in papers where the data have been subjected to a battery of several statistical tests. Of course, if we look hard enough, we can find statistically significant results in any data. Try a simple exercise: find a group of ten men and a group of ten women, and get them to write down their house numbers. Then trawl through the results looking for interesting findings. Does one group contain significantly more even numbers than the other? Are prime numbers much commoner in one group than the other? Does one group have significantly more three-digit numbers than the other? Go on searching till you find an interesting-looking result.

What does the result prove about sex differences in house numbers for the general population? Not much! How then did you manage to come up with such significant findings? The answer is that you searched through the data set picking out the ways in which it happened to look interesting, instead of deciding what you were going to look for in advance of collecting the data. Of course, if you search for the patterns that are there by coincidence in your particular data, you will find something that looks interesting. Authors are sometimes tempted to go on 'fishing expeditions', trawling through their data to find an apparently significant result. Readers should look out for suspicious clues:

- large numbers of comparisons between samples or subgroups: for example, tests for many different endpoints, tests that involve splitting the sample into many subgroups, or tests performed at many time points;
- a statistically significant result for an outcome that was not one of the stated objectives of the research;
- the appearance of statistical significance in tests designed after the data were collected (*post hoc* analysis);
- a result for which no clear scientific hypothesis is given.

You may be tempted to wonder, for example, whether Gene MacHine really had any valid scientific reason to compare northern Europe with Mediterranean Europe. His results, he assures us, are statistically significant; but do they mean anything?

Paper in focus

MacMahon, B., Yen, S., Trichopoulos, D., Warren, K. and Nardi, G. (1981) 'Coffee and cancer of the pancreas', *New Engl. J. Med.* 304: 630–3.

Over the past few decades, cancer of the pancreas has emerged as one of the most important neoplasias in human beings . . .. Causative factors have been sought in several previous studies, but only cigarette smoking has emerged as a consistent, though relatively weak, exogenous risk factor. We report the results of a study that was planned to reevaluate the relation of this disease to smoking and to examine the role of alcohol consumption as a possible confounding variable. Data were also obtained on intake of tea and coffee . . .

Several questions in the interview probed the duration and intensity of smoking of cigarettes, cigars and pipes. Questions on alcoholic beverages asked about the frequency of use before the onset of illness, the age span over which such use occurred, and the type of beverage used most frequently. The questions on tea and coffee were limited to the number of cups consumed in a typical day before the current illness was evident . . .

Among men, the relative risk associated with use of cigars . . . was 1.0 [suggesting that smoking cigars carries exactly the same risk for pancreatic cancer as not smoking cigars] . . . and that with use of a pipe was 1.0 . . .

The data on use of cigarettes are shown in Table 1. There was a weak positive association . . .

Table 2 shows a comparison of use of alcoholic beverages by cases [people with pancreatic cancer] and by controls [without pancreatic cancer]. No notable or significant association appeared . . .

The tea consumption of cases and controls is shown in Table 3. A slight inverse association appeared in both sexes, but it was not significant in either.

An unexpected association of pancreatic cancer with coffee consumption was evident (Table 4). Among men, each category of coffee consumption had a statistically significant excess risk as compared with that of nondrinkers of coffee . . .

Here, associations have been sought for pancreatic cancer with cigar smoking, pipe smoking, cigarette smoking, alcohol and tea as well as coffee – quite a line-up of tests. The investigation was originally intended to be about smoking and alcohol in relation to pancreatic cancer. This is an important point, because the study was specifically designed for that purpose, for example by excluding controls who had diseases known to be associated with smoking or alcohol consumption, and by asking rather detailed questions about smoking and alcohol consumption but only a sketchy one about coffee-drinking. Some aspects of the study design were therefore not ideal for an investigation of coffee, and may have biased the results. None of this *proves* that the results were artefactual, but there are certainly grounds for questioning their reliability.

Several features of this paper assist the reader. The authors state from the outset that they were not originally investigating coffee as a risk factor. They publish their negative results. They warn that the association they have found does not in itself implicate coffee as a causative agent of pancreatic cancer. Unfortunately, not all papers are this forthright. In particular, authors may publish only their 'positive' results and we may never get to hear about large numbers of statistical tests that did not give statistically significant results.

☞ Fishing expeditions may produce artefactual significant results

Authors who perform multiple comparisons between data sets can reassure us that they have tried to guard against chance findings. Helpful pointers include:

- a statement that the tests to be done were decided before data analysis started;
- a correction to the level of statistical significance that will be considered noteworthy – in other words, an increase in stringency. Often, researchers count results as statistically significant only if they have a P value less than 5% (or whatever level of significance they would demand for a single comparison) *divided by the number of comparisons*. For example, if investigators are doing ten comparisons between the same groups, they may choose not to report a given result as statistically significant unless it reaches significance at the 0.5% level, i.e. unless P ≤ 0.005.

Confidence intervals

Any statistic such as the mean value in a sample or the difference between two sample means is an estimate of something. The mean height in a sample of people is an estimate of the mean height in the whole population. The difference in mean times to recover from a cold between a sample taking treatment and a sample taking placebo is an estimate of the underlying difference in mean recovery time given very large populations in which the mean time to recovery is stable. Of course, our estimate is subject to statistical variation and we cannot be confident that it represents the 'true' value exactly. One limitation of P values is that they tell us nothing about the reliability of our estimates.

Confidence intervals measure how close our results are likely to be to the 'true' value. A confidence interval is a range of values within which the quantity we are interested in has a specified chance of lying – often a chance of at least 95%. The interval will contain our estimate of the quantity, plus a range of values somewhat above and somewhat below it.

For example, Lancaster *et al.* (1999) studied people who wished to give up smoking. The investigators measured the proportion of people who managed to give up for a sustained period after receiving brief advice from their doctor, and compared it to the proportion who managed to give up after receiving the same advice supplemented with extended counselling by a nurse. They found that brief advice plus counselling was no more effective than brief advice alone, and reported the results as follows: '[t]he proportion showing sustained abstinence was 3.6% in the extended counselling group, and 4.4% in the brief advice group (difference = −0.8%; 95% confidence interval = −4.3% to 2.6%).' In the samples studied, advice plus extended counselling was marginally *less* effective than brief advice alone (hence the difference of *minus* 0.8%); and the researchers were 95% certain that the true difference in the percentages of people quitting after the two interventions lies between –4.3% (4.3% fewer quitters in the counselling group) and 2.6% (2.6% more quitters in the counselling group).

The width of a confidence interval depends on how confident we want to be that the value we are estimating lies within the interval. For example, 99% confidence intervals are wider than 95% confidence intervals: if we want an interval to have a 99% chance of containing the real value rather than only a 95% chance, we had better make the interval larger. Similarly, 90% confidence intervals are narrower than 95% confidence intervals.

The main advantage of confidence intervals is that they focus attention on the actual scientific or clinical result, and away from the unhelpful 'significant'/'not significant' dichotomy. A difference in recovery times between drug and placebo together with an associated confidence interval allows us to think about *how much* difference there is between treatments and how *clinically* significant that difference is, rather than concentrating purely on *whether* there is a difference and asking whether it reaches *statistical* significance.

☞ Confidence intervals help us interpret statistics realistically

As we have described, confidence intervals are about taking the effects of random variation into account. In the face of this random variation, statistical analysis gives us some indication of the precision of our results. It is important to note that statistical measures do *not* say anything about the presence of systematic biases, only about the likely effect of chance. For example, imagine that in the smoking cessation study we have quoted, the investigators had determined whether people had given up smoking simply by asking them. Two types of unreliability would have affected the results. First, the samples of patients may not have been representative of the whole population because of the effects of chance. Confidence intervals express the uncertainty arising from such random variation. Second, the results may have been biased in the direction of overestimating cessation frequency, because people tend to claim that they have given up even when they have not. No amount of statistical analysis can take account of such bias. (In real life, the researchers were aware of this problem, and so did not use simple questioning on its own to determine whether their subjects had given up smoking.)

Sample size

The usual way to get round variability in measurements is to perform an experiment several times so that we can base the conclusions on several measurements. This gives us a better idea of the quantity that we are looking at than one measurement alone; it also gives us some idea of how variable the quantity is. Furthermore, if we make a significant error on one measurement, it will cause serious problems if that is the only measurement we have, but will not affect the results so badly if we have many other measurements of the same quantity.

What do you think of Gene MacHine's results? One reading for one flavour seems to have been wildly out of kilter with all the others. Was the experiment repeated enough times to show whether the high reading was part of the normal variation or a one-off mistake?

☞ **Measurements should be repeated an adequate number of times**

Multiple measurements in science often involve repeating an experiment or performing several experiments in parallel. In clinical trials, a frequent design is to give an experimental treatment to one sample of subjects and a control treatment to another sample. Statistical tests tell us whether the samples are sufficiently large. If samples are small, any difference between them is unlikely to reach statistical significance (unless the difference is very marked). The danger with small samples is thus that a genuine but modest difference will be wrongly attributed to pure chance.

The probability that a study will detect a difference if it is really there is called the 'power' of the study. Several factors affect the power of a study.

- Power increases with sample size: the bigger the samples, the easier it is to find differences if they exist.
- Power increases with increasing disparity between the groups: the more marked the difference is, the more likely we are to spot it.
- Power decreases as we demand a higher level of statistical significance: it is harder to demonstrate a difference that is significant at the 1% level than it is to demonstrate a difference that is only significant at the 5% level.
- If we are looking at a continuous variable like height or quality of life, then the spread of the variable in each sample also affects the power. Power increases as spread decreases (see Figure 6.1).

Designers of clinical trials and other experiments need to decide what size of sample to use. Typically they do this by considering the various factors we have just discussed. They specify what size of difference they are interested in being able to find between groups; how certain they want to be of finding the difference if it is there (i.e. the power); the level of statistical significance at which they wish to demonstrate the difference; and their estimate of how variable the measured quantity will be in each group. Using these figures, they perform a 'power calculation' which tells them what sample size they need to use.

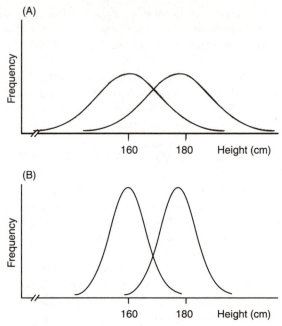

Figure 6.1 Two samples of people with mean heights of 160 cm and 180 cm. (A) the heights in each sample have a wide spread and the samples overlap a lot. The difference between samples is hard to demonstrate statistically. (B) the heights in each sample have a narrow spread and the samples do not overlap very much. The difference between samples is easy to demonstrate statistically.

Take this example from the smoking cessation paper: '[t]he sample size was calculated to detect, with 5% significance and 80% power, a 10% rate of sustained abstinence in the intensively counselled group. The assumed rate of sustained abstinence in the brief advice group was 3%. The target sample size was therefore 259 in each group.' The investigators wanted to be able to detect a 10% rate of sustained abstinence in the counselled group. This decision is based purely on a judgement about what level of quitting is clinically worth finding. They wanted to distinguish this 10% quit rate from an estimated 3% quit rate in the brief advice group. The only way to make such an estimate is to perform a small-scale pilot study, or to rely on similar studies in the published literature. In this case, the authors refer in their Introduction to previous studies suggesting a quit rate around 3% following brief advice alone. They wanted to be 80% certain of finding the specified difference if it really existed. The choice of 80% power is arbitrary but is commonly used in practice, although 90% is more usual. And they wanted to demonstrate their result at the 5% level of statistical significance. Again, the choice of 5% is arbitrary but very standard. On the basis of all these figures, the researchers calculated that they needed a minimum of 259 people in each group.

What is the point of knowing all this detail if you are not actually designing an experiment? Surely we can rely on researchers to do the calculations correctly? It transpires that quite a lot of studies end up under-powered, that is, too small to have a good chance of detecting the specified degree of difference at the specified level of significance. Readers need to understand the reasons for this problem and to look out for it. Furthermore, in some studies, no power calculation is reported. In these cases, we are entitled to wonder whether researchers have given enough consideration to their sample sizes at the outset. An example is the paper on treating eczema and psoriasis that we discussed at the end of the previous chapter. The paper finds no significant difference between two treatment regimens, but does not discuss power. This means that we do not know how likely we would be to find a significant difference even if it does exist, and how likely we would be to miss it.

How can studies be under-powered if it is relatively easy to work out the required sample size? Several factors may conspire to reduce a study's power:

- It is usually difficult and always expensive to recruit enough people to participate. It is also unethical to use large numbers of human or animal subjects when a good result can be obtained with smaller numbers. Researchers are therefore under pressure to plan for the smallest possible sample sizes. They may be over-optimistic about the magnitude of any difference they expect to find between groups, or about how small the spread of values will be, because this allows planned sample size to be decreased. Smaller sample sizes mean experiments that are easier to carry out and more likely to receive funding. But when the experiment is conducted, the difference between the groups may turn out to be less than predicted, or the spread of values within each group may be greater than predicted. Both these effects will decrease the power of the study.

- People inevitably drop out of studies before they are finished, for all sorts of reasons. They may become ill, move house or simply decide that they do not wish to continue. Because of the pressures to minimise sample size, researchers may underestimate the number of drop-outs they have to allow for.

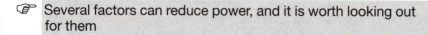 Several factors can reduce power, and it is worth looking out for them

Paper in focus

Sung, J.J.Y., Chung, S.C.S., Lai, C.-W., Chan, F.K.L., Leung, J.W.C., Yung, M.-Y., Kassianides, C. and Li, A.K.C. (1993) 'Octreotide infusion or emergency sclerotherapy for variceal haemorrhage', Lancet 342: 637–41.

The rupture of enlarged veins in the oesophagus – oesophageal varices – is a relatively common and potentially dangerous cause of bleeding in the upper gastrointestinal tract. Several emergency treatments are available to reduce bleeding, and this paper examines two of them. The first is intravenous infusion of octreotide, which decreases blood flow in the affected veins. The second is sclerotherapy, an injection into the affected vein of a substance (in this case sodium tetradecyl sulphate) that causes scarring and hence closure of the vein, ideally without damaging surrounding tissue. The procedure requires a good view of the oesophagus using an endoscope.

Based on an expected efficacy of 85% in the octreotide group and 90% in the sclerotherapy group (derived from our experience with sodium tetradecyl sulphate injection), with a two-tailed test to achieve a statistical power of 80% and a 5% [level of statistical significance], we estimated that at least 900 patients in each group were needed [i.e. 1800 altogether]. It is unlikely, therefore, that a clinical trial of a reasonable size can reach such a statistical power. We arbitrarily set a target of 100 patients [altogether] and accepted a chance of type II error [i.e. failure to find a difference that really exists] . . .

The overall success rate for endoscopic haemostasis [stopping of bleeding] was 90% for the sclerotherapy group and 84% for the octreotide group . . .

4 patients in the sclerotherapy group and 3 in the octreotide group died within 48h of admission (table 3). The overall hospital mortality was 27% in the sclerotherapy group and 20% in the octreotide group. The differences in 48-h mortality . . . and hospital mortality . . . were not significant . . .

Based on these endpoints [efficacy, mortality and some others not quoted in this extract], our study suggests that octreotide is as effective as endoscopic sclerotherapy and is a safe treatment for acute variceal bleeding.

Using a sample size of 50 in each group, the authors found efficacies for the two treatments (90% and 84%) that were extremely close to their predictions on the basis of past experience (90% and 85%). With very large samples, that relatively modest difference would have been statistically significant. But because the sample sizes here were so small, the difference was not statistically significant. The authors knew that, with small samples, there was a risk of missing a real difference (i.e. failing to find it completely or describing it as not statistically significant). In fact, for the samples described, that risk turns out to be over 85%.

The paper goes on to suggest that the treatments are equally efficacious. Do the findings really support that conclusion? As we have said, even if the treatments have slightly different efficacies as predicted, the study has more than an 85% chance of missing the difference. So failure to demonstrate a difference is not very strong evidence that there is no difference to find – only that the difference is too small to be demonstrated using such a small sample. Strictly speaking, a conclusion such as 'our study did not demonstrate a significant difference in efficacy between octreotide and sclerotherapy' would have been more precise.

The consequence of an under-powered study is decreased ability to find genuine effects. Given the pressures to lower sample size, it is not surprising that studies often end up with too little power to detect the specified effect. However, there is an ethical as well as a scientific problem with under-powering. Is it acceptable to put experimental subjects, human or animal, through a procedure that cannot give useful information? If it is completely clear that a study will not produce a meaningful result, people generally agree that it is unethical to carry it out. On the other hand, some studies are more or less forced to go ahead with limited power. Suppose that a study is set up to investigate the usefulness of a potential life-saving treatment for a rare disease. A hospital might wait ten years to get enough patients to do a study that has high power to detect a small but clinically meaningful effect. It may be preferable to go ahead and publish results after a couple of years if there seems to be a trend suggesting that the treatment is beneficial, even if the sample size is small and the power of the study low. The results should at least prompt further investigation, which might show that the effect was an artefact, but might also show that the treatment can save lives.

Similar considerations may have lain behind the decision to go ahead with the octreotide vs. sclerotherapy trial. As the authors explained, recruiting 900 patients in each group was difficult – it would have been necessary to wait a long time or perform the trial across a large number of hospitals. The value of the result is that it confirms that there is at least no very drastic difference between the treatments. Octreotide produced fewer serious short-term side effects than sclerotherapy, which is clearly a benefit. Octreotide is easier to use in certain cases, where bleeding is so heavy that it obscures the view at endoscopy, making sclerotherapy very difficult. The trial was useful in confirming that octreotide seems to be a safe and effective treatment for what can be a fatal condition, even if a detailed comparison with sclerotherapy is not warranted. Finally, small trials that are sufficiently similar can be aggregated and subjected to 'meta-analysis', which attempts to draw statistical conclusions from several pieces of work taken together. A piece of research can contribute to statistically significant findings on meta-analysis even if it contains no statistically significant results on its own. All these factors may have contributed to the decision to write up this study, and to the journal's decision to publish it, despite its low power.

THE SIGNIFICANCE OF FIGURES

Numerical analysis is not the only way of presenting data: papers also contain graphs, diagrams and photographs. These presentations, more than the words, contain the heart of the paper. In a graph or picture we can see the raw data in a format that allows us to make our own interpretation and does not confine us to the author's analysis. That is why it is important to read data as well as words.

Paper in focus

Werner, R. (1971) 'Mechanism of DNA replication', *Nature* 230: 570–2.

The figure below shows the incorporation of radioactive tritium into DNA. Some of the DNA ('heavy') is labelled with ^{13}C and ^{15}N, while some ('light') contains the commoner isotopes ^{12}C and ^{14}N. The total amount of heavy and light DNA is represented by the left- and right-hand peaks of the upper curve (filled circles). The distribution of tritium between the two types of DNA is represented by the lower curve (open circles). The experiment was designed to determine whether tritium was preferentially incorporated into light or heavy DNA, or whether it was incorporated equally into both. Since the tritium peak is directly between the two DNA peaks, tritium seems to be incorporated equally into light and heavy DNA. This is true for both part A of the figure (which represents small pieces of DNA) and part B (which represents large pieces). Although the tritium peak in part B inclines towards the left-hand, heavy DNA peak, this could just be due to the way that the curve has been drawn through the points: it is equally plausible that the true peak is symmetrical as in part A. In any case, if incorporation into heavy and light DNA were equal, one would expect more tritium towards the left of each diagram, since in both A and B the left-hand DNA peak is larger than the right.

The results of the experiment are described as follows in the text:

> Fig. 4 shows that nearly all the thymidine [the tritium-labelled compound] incorporated into both large and small DNA is covalently connected to heavy . . . DNA.

The text alone states a clear conclusion. Yet it is not so clear how the results shown in the figure support that conclusion.

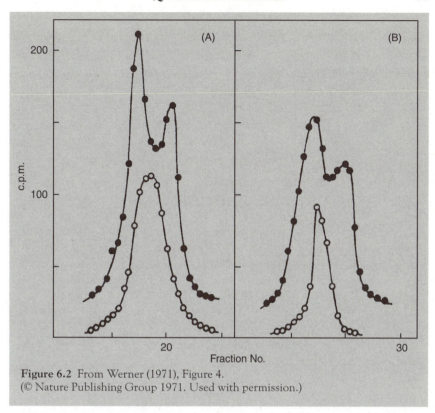

Figure 6.2 From Werner (1971), Figure 4.
(© Nature Publishing Group 1971. Used with permission.)

In Chapter 4, I suggested that we should be in the habit of evaluating results ourselves before reading the authors' conclusions. The results that we should scrutinise are the pictures, tables and graphs that show us what the authors saw (or at least those bits that the authors want us to see).

Papers in focus

Diederich, B., Wilkinson, J.F., Magnin, T., Najafi, S.M.A., Errington, J. and Yudkin, M.D. (1994) 'Role of interactions between SpoIIAA and SPoIIAB in regulating cell-specific transcription factor σ^F of *Bacillus subtilis*', *Genes Dev.* 8: 2653–63.

The figure shows the time course of an enzymatic reaction. Different reactions behave in different ways: some have an exponential time course, others a sigmoid one; still others show biphasic kinetics. The progress of the reaction over time gives important clues about the mechanism of the reaction. Here, the authors have joined their data points with a series of straight lines and have not attempted any analysis. Does your observation of the data suggest a particular time course?

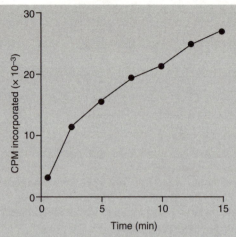

Figure 6.3 From Diederich *et al.* (1994), Figure 2d.
(© Cold Spring Harbor Laboratory 1994. Used with permission.)

Magnin, T., Lord, M. and Yudkin, M.D. (1997) 'Contribution of partner switching and SpoIIAA cycling to regulation of σ^F activity in sporulating *Bacillus subtilis*', *J. Bacteriol.* 179: 3922–7.

In this later paper, the same group has analysed the time course more fully, showing it to be biphasic.

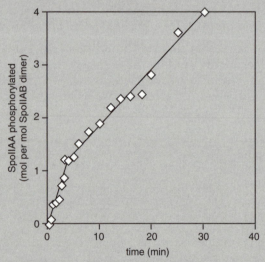

Figure 6.4 From Magnin *et al.* (1997), Figure 3.
(© American Society for Microbiology 1997. Used with permission.)

The authors go on to discuss at length the implications of the biphasic kinetics for the reaction mechanism.

A picture is worth a thousand words, according to the old cliché. Of course we need words to explain the figures in scientific papers – but as far as possible, the words should be our own.

 Figures show you the data without a heavy overlay of authorial interpretation

Summary

- Statistical significance is a useful measure, but does not prove that a result is either reliable or interesting.
- Multiple comparisons, *post hoc* analysis and inadequate attention to scientific plausibility are all risk factors for false positives.
- Statistics should be interpreted together with their confidence intervals and in the light of the sample sizes used.
- Figures and tables are an extremely significant part of a research paper: we should read them just as carefully as the words.

EXERCISE

The following extracts are from real papers. For each extract
1 comment on the strengths of the quantitative analysis;
2 comment on any weaknesses or limitations of the quantitative analysis, as far as you can tell from the quoted extract;
3 assess how well the text reflects the raw data where provided;
4 assess the scientific or clinical importance of the findings, as far as you can tell from the quoted extract;
5 suggest any points that you would expect to see discussed in the rest of the paper, or any further quantitative information that you would expect to find if you read the whole paper.

1. Patients were given a diary in which to record headache severity, associated symptoms [nausea, vomiting, aversion to light and aversion to sound], and functional disability immediately prior to taking the medication (0 hour) and again at 0.5, 1, 1.5, 2, 3, and 4 hours postdose . . .

    To investigate the higher than expected placebo response rates in this study, logistic regression models were used to analyze the potential effect of various factors on pain relief at 2 hours. The placebo response rate was found not to be influenced by aura, gender, [age], race, region, duration of typical headache, baseline severity, body mass index, or time of dosing during the day. An analysis examining treatment response in relation to the day of the week on which the 'study headache' occurred showed that more headaches occurred on Mondays than on any other day, and that fewer headaches occurred on Fridays, Saturdays and Sundays . . . . The analysis also showed that the placebo response rate (percent of subjects reporting pain relief at 2 hours) was lower on Saturdays (50%), Sundays (30%) and Mondays (50%) than on other days (greater than 62% with pain relief) . . .

The post hoc analyses performed to investigate the high placebo response rates yielded some interesting results. Most intriguingly, treatment with rizatriptan on weekends provided statistically superior relief (versus placebo), whereas weekday treatment did not . . .

From Winner, P., Lewis, D., Visser, W.H., Jiang, K., Ahrens, S. and Evans, J.K. (2002) 'Rizatriptan 5 mg for the acute treatment of migraine in adolescents: a randomized, double-blind, placebo-controlled study', *Headache* 42: 49–55.

2. We obtained positive PCR amplification using primers specific for p-35S [a transgenic piece of DNA not naturally present in maize] in five of the seven Mexican maize samples tested (Fig. 1). Four criollo samples [gathered from the wild, lanes **a–d**] showed weak albeit clear PCR amplification, whereas the Diconsa sample [provided by a governmental food distribution agency, lane **e**] yielded very strong amplification comparable in intensity to transgenic-positive Bt1 and RR1 controls [lanes **h** and **g**]. The historical negative control [harvested in 1971, before there was any transgenic maize] (data not shown) and the contemporary sample from Cuzco, Peru [harvested from a region where there is no transgenic maize growing nearby, lane **f**] were both invariably negative.

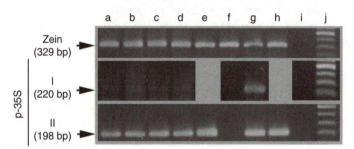

Figure 6.5 From Quist and Chapela (2001), Figure 1.
(© Nature Publishing Group 2001. Used with permission.)
From Quist, D. and Chapela, I.H. (2001) 'Transgenic DNA introgressed into traditional maize landraces in Oaxaca, Mexico', *Nature* 414: 541–3.

3. Otherwise healthy persons ages ≥ 13 years who presented with symptoms of influenza of ≤ 48 h duration were enrolled in the study . . ..
Symptoms of influenza were defined as feverishness and two or more of the following symptoms: myalgia, headache, cough, or sore throat . . .

Subjects [1256 in total] were randomized in the ratio 2:2:1:1 to receive one of the following treatments for 5 days: zanamivir, 10 mg 2×/day by oral inhalation plus 6.4 mg 2×/day by nasal spray; zanamivir, 10 mg 4×/day by oral inhalation plus 6.4 mg 4×/day by nasal spray; placebo by both routes 2×/day; or placebo by both routes 4×/day. Placebo groups were combined for analysis . . .

[Throat swabs taken on day 1 and blood samples taken on days 1 and 21 were analysed to find out whether symptoms were indeed caused by influenza.] Persons were defined as being influenza-positive if any of the following laboratory diagnostic tests had positive results: virus antigen detection, virus cell culture, or a 4-fold increase in anti-influenza antibody titer between days 1 and 21.

The calculation of sample size was based on the assumption that 50% of the intention-to-treat (ITT) population in the placebo group would have alleviation of clinically significant symptoms by day 5. A clinically relevant difference was defined as an increase to 65% of patients with alleviation of symptoms by day 5. A sample size of 720 patients (240/ group) is required for a two-tailed test of these proportions at the 5% level of significance and > 90% power . . .

For the overall ITT population, zanamivir reduced the median number of days to alleviation of clinically significant symptoms by 1 day compared with placebo (6 vs. 7 days; table 2). This difference was statistically significant for both zanamivir treatments ($P = .012$ 2×/day vs. placebo, $P = .014$ 4×/day vs. placebo). [Table 2 shows a difference in median time to recovery in placebo group vs. either of the zanamivir groups of 1.0 days, with 95% confidence interval 0.0–2.0 days].

Similar benefits (not shown) regarding symptom alleviation were seen in the corresponding analyses for the influenza-positive population. A reduction of 1.5 days in the time to symptom alleviation was seen in both zanamivir groups for the total influenza-positive population, although the differences were not statistically significant (5.5 vs. 7 days; $P = .11$ for zanamivir 2×/day, 95% CI, [−0.25, 2.0]; $P = .06$ for zanamivir 4×/ day, 95% CI, [0.0, 2.0]).

From Monto, A.S., Fleming, D.M., Henry, D., de Groot, R., Makela, M., Klein, T., Elliott, M., Keene, O.N. and Man, C.Y. (1999) 'Efficacy and safety of the neuraminidase inhibitor zanamivir in the treatment of influenza A and B virus infections', *J. Infect. Dis.* 180: 254–61.

4. We enrolled [207] children aged 1 to 15 years with mild or moderate atopic eczema within the past month. Children with severe eczema were excluded . . .

We randomised participants to one of two treatment groups. Children in the mild arm received 1% hydrocortisone ointment twice daily for seven days. Children in the potent arm used 0.1% betamethasone valerate . . . twice daily for three consecutive days, followed by a base emollient only (white soft paraffin) for four days. Both treatments were dispensed in white tubes labelled A and B to maintain blinding of the treatment allocation . . .

Primary outcomes were based on reports of scratching recorded in a daily diary. Scratch scores were graded in response to 'how much has your eczema made you scratch today?' from 1 (not at all) to 5 (all the time). Scores of 2 or less were categorised as a scratch-free period . . .

To detect a difference of at least 15% in the mean number of scratch-free days between the two groups, with an 0.05 two sided significance level and 90% power and an attrition rate of 10%, we needed 100 participants in each group . . .

The median number of scratch-free days was 118.0 for the mild group and 117.5 for the potent group (difference 0.5, 90% confidence interval −2.0 to 4.0; P = 0.53).

From Thomas, K.S., Armstrong, S., Avery, A., Li Wan Po, A., O'Neill, C., Young, S. and Williams, H.C. (2002) 'Randomised controlled trial of short bursts of a potent topical corticosteroid versus prolonged use of a mild preparation for children with mild or moderate atopic eczema', *BMJ* 324: 768–71.

5. As in other competitive sports, the famous Grand National steeple-chase . . . sometimes results in injury. By analysing data from the past 15 Grand National races (consisting of 560 starts by horses), we are able to identify several factors that are significantly associated with failure to complete the race . . .

Ground classified as 'soft' or 'heavy' resulted in a significantly higher rate of non-completion (hazard ratio, 2.05; 95% CI, 1.32, 3.17) compared with all other types. The model predicts that only 18% of runners will complete when the 'going' is soft or heavy (Fig. 2c) . . .

Falling or unseating of the jockey as a result of a jumping error is the outcome most likely to result in injury . . .. Horses with no previous experience on the course were at increased risk of falling and of losing their rider (hazard ratio, 2.6; 95% CI, 1.80, 3.87). Good-to-soft ground was associated with a significantly decreased risk of falling relative to good ground (hazard ratio, 0.41; 95% CI, 0.21, 0.78) . . .

From Proudman, C., Pinchbeck, G., Clegg, P. and French, N. (2004) 'Risk of horses falling in the Grand National', *Nature* 428: 385–6.

6. During the immediate-early response of mammalian cells to mitogens, histone H3 is rapidly and transiently phosphorylated by one or more unidentified kinases. [This paper presents evidence that a kinase called] Rsk-2 . . . was required for epidermal growth factor (EGF)-stimulated phosphorylation of H3 . . .

. . . we specifically disrupted the *RSK-2* gene in murine embryonic stem (ES) cells by homologous recombination and assayed these cells for EGF-stimulated phosphorylation of histone H3. The absence of Rsk-2 expression in these cells was confirmed by protein immunoblotting (Fig. 6A) . . . . Augmented phosphorylation of H3 was detected . . . after EGF stimulation of serum-deprived wild-type (wt) ES cells (Fig. 6B). In contrast, no stimulation of H3 phosphorylation in response to EGF was detected in Rsk-2⁻ cells . . . (Fig. 6B) . . .

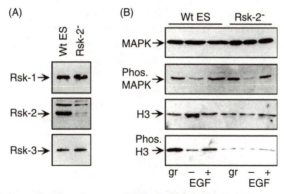

Figure 6.6 From Sassone-Corsi *et al.* (1999), Figure 6A and B.
(Reprinted with permission from Sassone-Corsi, P. *et al.* (1999) *Science* 285:
886–91, © 1999 AAAS.)

Figure 6 Rsk-2 is required for EGF-stimulated phosphorylation of
histone H3 in mouse cells. **(A)** . . . wild-type (wt ES) and Rsk-2 deficient
(Rsk-2⁻) cells were starved for 48 hours . . . and then stimulated with
EGF . . . for 30 min . . . . Expression of Rsk-1, Rsk-2 and Rsk-3 was
then analyzed by immunoblotting . . . **(B)** Samples prepared as in (A)
from serum-deprived (–EGF) and EGF-stimulated (+EGF) wild-type and
Rsk2⁻ . . . cells were resolved on a 10% SDS-PAGE gel, and the levels of
MAPK . . ., phosphorylated MAPK, H3, and phosphorylated H3 were
assessed by immunoblotting with the respective antisera . . . . EGF stimulated MAPK phosphorylation in both wt and Rsk2⁻ cells. The levels of
(nonphosphorylated) H3 and MAPK confirm equivalent loading.
From Sassone-Corsi, P., Mizzen, C.A., Cheung, P., Crosio, C., Monaco, L., Jacquot,
   S., Hanauer, A. and Allis, C.D. (1999) 'Requirement of Rsk-2 for epidermal growth
   factor-activated phosphorylation of histone H3', *Science* 285: 886–91.

7. Allergic rhinitis is the most common form of allergic disease, estimated
   to affect up to 20% of the population worldwide . . .
   The cysteinyl leukotriene type-1 (CysLT1) receptor antagonist montelukast . . . has been documented to significantly improve symptoms of
   seasonal allergic rhinitis . . . the primary objective of this study was to
   test the efficacy of montelukast 10 mg administered once daily in the
   morning to patients with seasonal allergic rhinitis . . .
   Loratadine, an antihistamine, served as the positive control to validate
   the study . . .
   When examined week by week, montelukast was significantly more
   effective than placebo in improving daytime nasal, night-time, daytime
   eye, and composite symptom scores at every week (Fig. 3). In contrast,
   the treatment effect of loratadine by week, compared with placebo,
   tended to decrease throughout the study. To evaluate the time course
   of the treatment effect, an analysis of the slope of the mean change
   from baseline by week was performed for all 4 weeks. The difference

in slopes between montelukast and placebo was −0.01/week for each
of the daytime, night-time, daytime eye, and composite symptom
scores, and was not significant, indicating a constant treatment effect
greater than the placebo effect. In contrast, the difference in slopes
between loratadine and placebo for the secondary endpoints ranged
from 0.01 to 0.03/week (P = not significant) and was 0.04/week for the
primary endpoint of daytime nasal symptoms score (P=0.036), indicating a diminishing loratadine treatment effect for the primary
endpoint.

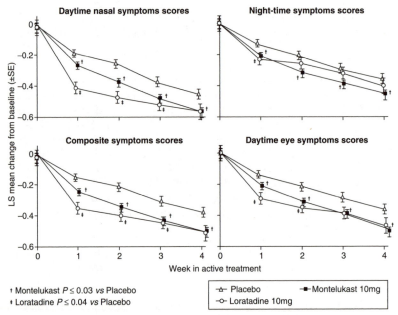

Figure 6.7 From van Adelsberg et al. (2003), Figure 3. [LS, least squares]
(© Blackwell Publishing 2003. Used with permission.)
From van Adelsberg, J., Philip, G., Pedinoff, A.J., Meltzer, E.O., Ratner, P.H., Menten, J.
and Reiss, T.F. (2003) 'Montelukast improves symptoms of seasonal allergic rhinitis
over a 4-week treatment period', Allergy 58: 1268–76.

8. Pregnancy itself, regardless of ultrasound examinations, is in many
women associated with psychological stress and anxiety (4,5). These
problems are most apparent during the first trimester, while they seem to
decrease in mid-pregnancy and increase again during the last trimester
(6–8). Studies on women's worries during pregnancy have shown that the
baby's health was the most important concern (5,8,9). Considering this
state of increased vulnerability during pregnancy, it is reasonable to
assume that an intervention aiming at looking for fetal abnormalities may
affect women's anxiety . . .

Therefore, the aim of this study was to evaluate the effects of fetal ultrasound screening for Down's syndrome in a low-risk population on women's anxiety, specifically on women's worries about something being wrong with the baby, in mid-pregnancy and 2 months after delivery . . .

The power calculation was based on figures from an English survey showing that 22% of the women were worried about the fetus in mid-pregnancy and 23% in late pregnancy (8). Women's worries about the 'possibility of something being wrong with the baby' were measured by the Cambridge Worry Scale including 16 items of common concerns during pregnancy. In order to detect a clinically significant increase by 25% of women who were worried about the health of the fetus from the expected 23% in the routine ultrasound group to 29% in the early ultra-sound group [80% power, 95% confidence interval (CI)], 840 women were required in each group. To detect a reduction of the same size, from 23% to 17%, 700 women would be required in each group. After taking non-responders into account, the final sample was estimated at 2000 women with 1000 in each group.

From Öhman, S.G., Saltvedt, S., Grunewald, C. and Waldenström, U. (2004) 'Does fetal screening affect women's worries about the health of their baby? A random-ized controlled trial of ultrasound screening for Down's syndrome versus routine ultrasound screening', *Acta Obstet. Gynecol. Scand.* 83: 634–40.

9. [The gorilla may be a threatened species. Criteria for judging a species' vulnerability are debated, and the original criteria have been changed, so] now seems a good time both to reassess the conservation status of *Gorilla gorilla*, and to test the applicability of the latest . . . draft criteria with a worked example. If the criteria cannot be applied to a species as well known as is the gorilla, then they are probably inapplicable to most species . . .

To calculate an upper estimate of the total number of gorillas in Africa, I multiplied the extent of 'closed forest' (indicative of gorilla habitat) within the gorilla's geographic range by 0.25. This value of 0.25 gorillas/km² falls between the values of 0.18/km² for suitable habitat in Gabon (Tutin & Fernandez, 1984) and 0.4/km² for Congo (Fay & Agnagna, 1992). The intermediate value results in a total number of gorillas for Gabon that is at the upper limit of the Tutin and Fernandez estimate of numbers. Fay and Agnagna did not give an estimate of total numbers of gorillas, but my total calculated by use of the density value 0.25 agrees with their implication that the Congo's numbers matched Gabon's. Thus it seems as if the 0.25 value might be within limits of accuracy. In conservation areas, I assumed a density of 0.5 gorilla/km², although 1.0 gorilla/km² is not unrealistic, especially if gorillas are squeezed at unusually high densities into remaining conservation areas [several references are provided].

Values for extent of closed forest (also called moist forest) were taken from Sayer *et al.* (1992) and World Resources Institute (1992). Certainly

many questions surround the reliability of any figures on extent of
forest and its rate of disappearance . . .. However, Skole and Tucker's
(1993) assessment for the Amazon indicates that they could be of the
order of magnitude of accuracy necessary for assessment of IUCN
[World Conservation Union] conservation status. In addition, 'closed
forest' will exclude some gorilla habitats, but at the same time it will
probably also include non-habitat . . .

A usable index of the potential for decline in gorilla habitat could . . .
be national rates of disappearance of 'closed/moist forest' . . .. While
the figures' reliability has been criticised, especially for their potential
exaggeration of the gravity of destruction, Skole and Tucker's (1993)
analysis indicates that the knock-on effects of deforestation – provision
of access to settlers, for instance – can be so detrimental that the exag-
gerations reflect reality . . .

From Harcourt, A.H. (1996) 'Is the gorilla a threatened species? How should we
judge?', *Biol. Cons.* 75: 165–76.

10. Individual susceptibility to toxic effects can be caused by reduced DNA
repair capacity which can either be due to genetic predisposition or
to interference with the repair process by extraneous substances . . ..
The latter phenomenon can be tested using the challenge assay . . . the
rationale for the assay is that cells from exposed individuals will
have impaired DNA repair activities. When these cells are challenged
by X rays in vitro, they will make mistakes in the repair of the X ray-
induced DNA strand breaks, resulting in a significant increase of
chromosome aberrations compared with cells from non-exposed
individuals . . .

Fourteen styrene-exposed boat builders (6419 cells scored) of a small
shipyard and seven controls (3505 cells scored) from a training center
for the wood manufacturing industry were investigated for CA
[chromosome aberrations] . . .. The challenge assay was used to measure interference with DNA repair in the exposed boat builders (4440
cells scored). Due to an experimental mistake a wrong irradiation time
was chosen for the control samples. Hence, unfortunately, they could
not be used for comparison with the exposed workers. Results were
therefore compared between different exposure levels within the
exposed group and stratified for lifetime exposure and age. A historical
control consisting of two persons from our institute (573 cells scored)
was available but for principal methodological reasons comparisons can
only be exploratory . . .

Fourteen workers exposed to low levels of styrene . . . and seven
controls were investigated for baseline structural chromosome aberrations using FISH. A slightly higher rate of exchange-type aberrations /
100 cells in exposed 0.22 (95% CI, 0.13–0.36) compared to controls
0.14 (95% CI, 0.05–0.31) was observed (Table 1). The difference
between the rates was not statistically significant.

After X-ray challenge the rates of exchange-type aberrations were

13.26 (10.53–16.50) in the historical control and 16.19 (15.00–17.40) in the exposed group (Table 2). The difference was statistically significant (p < 0.038) in a right sided Fisher's exact test based on 719 exchanges in 4440 metaphases in the exposed group and 79 exchanges in 573 metaphases in the historical controls (Table 2).

From Oberheitmann, B., Frentzel-Beyme, R. and Hoffmann, W. (2001) 'An application of the challenge assay in boat builders exposed to low levels of styrene – a feasibility study of a possible biomarker for acquired susceptibility', *Int. J. Hyg. Environ. Health* 204: 23–9.

11. Definitive diagnosis of *Schistosoma mansoni* infection requires the demonstration of eggs in faeces . . .. The Kato–Katz method is currently the choice for parasitological diagnosis . . .. However, the sensitivity of parasitological methods diminishes when prevalence and intensity of infection are low . . .. In addition, parasitological methods are not sufficient for diagnosis of recent infections in which worms have not yet started to produce eggs . . .. To address these shortcomings, antibody detection methods have been evaluated as adjuncts to faecal examinations . . .

All individuals received 3 vials to collect faeces during 3 consecutive days identified by name and registration number. Parasitological examination was performed using the quantitative method of Kato–Katz . . .. The arithmetic mean of 3 faecal samples was considered as the individual egg output value.

Two different commercial kits for collection of oral fluid were tested . . .. For saliva, the cotton pad was inserted under the tongue and for oral transudate the cotton pad was placed between the cheek and inferior gum . . . [the oral transudate kit was eventually chosen] . . .

[*S. mansoni* eggs produce an antigen, *S. mansoni* egg antigen (SAE), against which infected individuals produce an antibody, anti-SAE IgG. The levels of this antibody were measured by ELISA, which involves measuring the optical density of a solution]. The optical densities were measured at 405 nm . . .. All sera were tested in duplicate and each plate contained a positive control, consisting of a pool of 5 positive sera, and a negative control, consisting of 5 negative sera. The cut-off of each sample assay was based on the mean absorbancy of the negative control plus twice its standard deviation . . .

[Levels of antibody, as measured by ELISA, were compared with levels of active infection, as measured by eggs in faeces.]

Quantitative methods

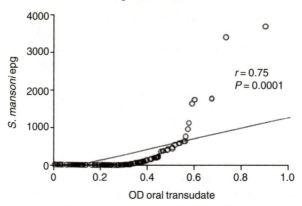

Figure 6.8 From Garcia Santos *et al.* (2000), Figure 2a.
(© Royal Society of Tropical Medicine and Hygiene 2000. Used with permission.)

Fig. 2. Correlation between anti-SEA IgG levels in oral transudate and numbers of eggs per gram of faeces . . .. IgG levels were determined by ELISA, with optical density (OD) read at 405 nm.

From Garcia Santos, M.M.A., Garcia, T.C., Orsini, M., Disch, J., Katz, N. and Rabello, A. (2000) 'Oral fluids for the immunodiagnosis of *Schistosoma mansoni* infection', *Trans. Roy. Soc. Trop. Med. Hyg.* 94: 289–92.

12. For Scatchard analysis, cultures were seeded at an initial density of 1×10^6 cells/ml in 150-mm dishes, and treated with RA [retinoic acid] (10^{-6} M). Three days later, binding of ^{125}I-labeled NGF [nerve growth factor] (3 pM to 3 nM) to intact cells (0.5×10^6 cells/ml) was measured using the sucrose sedimentation protocol (49). Nonspecific binding of ^{125}I-labeled NGF was determined by the addition of 1 mM unlabeled NGF . . .. All determinations were done in triplicates and data are presented as mean ± S.E . . .

To determine whether RA increases the binding of NGF to PC12 cells, we performed Scatchard plot analysis of the binding of ^{125}I-labeled NGF to control PC12 cells and cells treated with RA . . . PC12 cells contained high-affinity receptors ($K_d = 3.8 \pm 1.6 \times 10^{-11}$ M) and low-affinity receptors ($K_d = 1.2 \pm 0.1 \times 10^{-9}$ M; Fig. 4). Pretreatment with RA (10^{-6} M) resulted in an approximate 3-fold increase in the number of low-affinity binding sites (from $4.3 \pm 1.2 \times 10^4$ to $12.6 \pm 1.8 \times 10^4$ sites/cell; Fig. 4) without causing a significant change in the high-affinity sites ($3.6 \pm 0.5 \times 10^3$ to $3.6 \pm 0.4 \times 10^3$ sites/cell; Fig. 4).

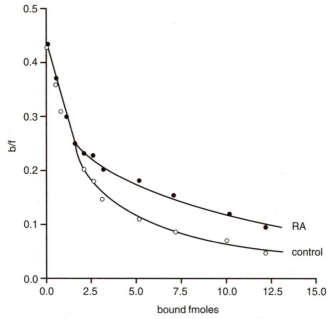

Figure 6.9 From Scheibe and Wagner (1992), Figure 4.
(© American Society for Biochemistry and Molecular Biology 1992. Used with permission.)

Fig. 4. Scatchard plot of specific NGF binding to RA-treated PC12 cells. PC12 cells were incubated in the presence and absence of RA (10^{-6} M). Three days later the binding of ^{125}I-labeled NGF(3 pM to 3 nM) to cells (0.5×10^6 cells/ml) was measured at 4°C for 90 min as described under 'Experimental Procedures.'

From Scheibe, R.J. and Wagner, J.A. (1992) 'Retinoic acid regulates both expression of the nerve growth factor receptor and sensitivity to nerve growth factor', *J. Biol. Chem.* 267: 17611–16.

13. Secondary hyperparathyroidism is common in end stage renal disease and may cause disabling bone problems, growth retardation, and other complications. [Decreasing the amount of phosphate ingested or absorbed can suppress this condition.] Very low phosphate diets are unpalatable, and oral aluminium compounds used to bind dietary phosphate to prevent absorption carry a risk of aluminium toxicity, particularly in young children . . .. Calcium carbonate has been used as an alternative phosphate binder . . .. We studied the use of high dose phosphate binders and mild dietary phosphate restriction for the suppression of secondary hyperparathyroidism and compared aluminium hydroxide and calcium carbonate as phosphate binders . . .

   Twelve children aged 5–15 years (mean 11 years) in stable chronic renal failure were studied . . .

. . . the diet was stabilised with moderate phosphorus restriction while maintaining protein intake . . .. Food tables were given so that food items with a low phosphorus content could be chosen . . .

The patients were randomly allocated to receive either aluminium hyroxide or calcium carbonate as the phosphate binder. The dosage was increased to reduce the plasma phosphate concentration to the lower limit of the normal range and the children were seen fortnightly until this was achieved . . .

Parathyroid hormone concentrations were reduced to within the normal range for children (less than $450\,ng/l$) by the end of six months of treatment . . .

The biochemical changes at the end of six months of treatment with either calcium carbonate or aluminium hydroxide were not significantly different apart from higher serum aluminium concentrations during treatment with aluminium hydroxide . . .

Side effects included transient periods of hypercalcaemia and hypo-phosphataemia, which were easily reversed by reducing the dosage of phosphate binder. There was no significant difference in the incidence of side effects during treatment with calcium carbonate or aluminium hydroxide. . ..

Calcium carbonate was as effective as aluminium hydroxide as a phosphate binder and an improvement in growth was noted. The regimen was well tolerated with few and easily reversible side effects. In view of the risk of aluminium toxicity we recommend that high dose calcium carbonate should be used as the phosphate binder in patients with chronic renal failure . . .

From Mak, R.H.K., Turner, C., Thompson, T., Powell, H., Haycock, G.B. and Chantler, C. (1985) 'Suppression of secondary hyperparathyroidism in children with chronic renal failure by high dose phosphate binders: calcium carbonate versus aluminium hydroxide', Brit. Med. J. 291: 623–7.

14. The aim of this study was to investigate the dose-response dependency of cutaneous nickel allergic reactions in nickel-sensitive individuals exposed to a high dose of nickel and to oral nickel doses within the range of nickel exposure from the normal daily diet in a double-blind, placebo-controlled trial . . .

[t]he 40 nickel-sensitive individuals were randomly divided into 4 groups and orally exposed in a double-blind fashion to 0.3, 1.0 or 4.0 mg nickel . . . in a lactose capsule or just lactose as placebo . . .. A nickel exposure dose of 0.3 mg is close to the estimated average nickel intake from the normal daily diet. A 1.0 mg nickel dose . . . has been estimated to be close to the possible maximum nickel intake from the daily diet (12). Exposure to 4.0 mg nickel was expected to result in flare-up reactions in most of the nickel-sensitive individuals and was therefore included as a positive control. The 20 healthy controls were randomly divided into 2 groups and exposed orally in a double-blind fashion to 4.0 mg nickel or a placebo . . .

7 of 10 nickel-sensitive individuals had cutaneous reactions to the oral exposure to 4.0 mg nickel, 4 reacted to 1.0 mg, 4 had a reaction to 0.3 mg and 1 nickel-sensitive individual reacted to a placebo . . .. No one in the control group had a cutaneous reaction to any of the oral exposures. The frequency of reactions among nickel-sensitive volunteers exposed to 4.0 mg nickel was statistically significantly different from the frequencies in the group given a placebo ($P = 0.0099$) and from the equivalent control group ($P = 0.0015$). None of the other pair-wise comparisons showed a statistically significant difference ($P > 0.05$) . . .

The limited number of persons exposed in each group ($n = 10$ per group) may explain why no statistically significant differences were found between the nickel-sensitive individuals exposed to 1.0 or 0.3 mg nickel and those given a placebo. Assuming the frequencies found in this study are correct, a power-calculation (power $\geq 80\%$, significance level $P = 5\%$) found that each group had to include 36 volunteers to demonstrate statistically significant differences between the groups of nickel-sensitive volunteers exposed to 1.0 mg nickel or 0.3 mg nickel and the group given a placebo . . .. Of course, an extrapolation of the results found among a low number of individuals . . . to a larger number would be statistically incorrect . . .

From Jensen, C.S., Menné, T., Lisby, S., Kristiansen, J. and Veien, N.K. (2003) 'Experimental systemic contact dermatitis from nickel: a dose-response study', *Contact Dermatitis* 49: 124–32.

REFERENCES

Irnich, D., Behrens, N., Molzen, H., König, A., Gleditsch, J., Krauss, M., Natalis, M., Senn, E., Beyer, A. and Schöps, P. (2001) 'Randomised trial of acupuncture compared with conventional massage and "sham" laser acupuncture for treatment of chronic neck pain', *BMJ* 322: 1574–9.

Lancaster, T., Dobbie, W., Vos, K., Yudkin, P., Murphy, M. and Fowler, G. (1999) 'Randomized trial of nurse-assisted strategies for smoking cessation in primary care', *Brit. J. Gen. Pract.* 49: 191–4.

7

Thinking science

Discussion

Griddle and Byrne (2002) tested radicullin for its ability to induce mutations in the bacterium *Salmonella typhimurium* TA98 and found 2,100 revertants per microgram in a standard Ames test. It is well known that most mutagens are also carcinogenic, and it is therefore probable that radicullin causes cancer in humans.

Given the importance of tastie root as a foodstuff in Europe, we re-examined the correlation between estimated tastie root consumption and a variety of cancers on that continent. Lyse, Damlise and Statz (2001) found a striking correlation between tastie root consumption and death rates from liver cancer in seven European countries. Omitting France from their data set gives an even higher linear correlation between per capita consumption of tastie root and liver cancer deaths in the remaining six countries. We suspect that other factors in the French diet may protect against the carcinogenic effects of tastie root.

Dietary factors (e.g. aflatoxin) are known to play a part in carcinogenesis. Despite a European initiative beginning in the mid-1980s to reduce cancer mortality, about 10% more people died from cancer in the European Union in 2000 than in 1985, so the study of dietary risk factors is timely and important.

We have demonstrated a radicullin level of up to 0.8 ng/g in samples of Radichips. Since the estimated consumption of tastie root in Europe is 48 kg per capita, the intake of radicullin could be as high as 38.4 µg per person per year – several hundred times higher than the maximum tolerable annual intake of dioxins recommended by the US Environmental Protection Agency.

Changing food habits is a formidable challenge (Stodji and Karbs, 1985). However, our discovery of a potent mutagen in such a widely-consumed staple does pose serious questions about the safety of European diets, particularly outside France. We suggest that strenuous efforts be made to decrease the use of tastie root where at all possible.

Professor Stickler began to sob quietly to herself. It had been a long, long time, she reflected, since she had been reduced to tears by a paper – or by anything else for that matter. As the red pen rolled from her hand and plopped onto the office floor, her thoughts drifted to Bermuda. There would surely be plenty of people at the conference who would be glad of a nice young man to help them around the lab. That was exactly the problem, she realised: Gene MacHine was so nice, so very very *nice*. If only she could persuade . . .. Professor Stickler brightened a little as she thought which of her eminent colleagues she would most like to donate him to. It would only be fair, she decided, to write him an exceedingly good reference.

ASSUMPTIONS AND DEDUCTIONS

Good methods can provide valuable results, but even the most reliable results do not mean anything until they are interpreted. No matter how carefully I measure something and how rigorously I exclude confounding variables, if I misinterpret what I have seen, my conclusions will be questionable.

Outside the box

One difficult thing about interpreting observations is spotting that the obvious interpretation is not necessarily the right one. Indeed, even noticing that alternatives exist can be very hard. For nobody is it harder than for the researchers themselves. If I set up an experiment to test a hypothesis; if I expect a particular result; if I see just that result and it makes perfect sense in the framework of my expectation – then how am I supposed to leap outside my mental space and come up with a different possibility?

To be sure, this is what we expect scientists to do all the time. The art of being a good researcher includes the facility to scrutinise one's own results, to come up with various possible interpretations and to perform additional experiments that try to distinguish between them. Most scientific papers contain reasoning of this kind, often very ingeniously done. But given the difficulty of thinking in this way, it is not surprising that some papers manage it less perfectly than others. Is Gene MacHine, for example, right to assume that the levels of radicullin in deep-fried Radichips are the same as the levels in boiled tastie root, the form normally eaten in Europe? And is he right to compare Radichips with the vegetable char-grilled by Griddle and

Byrne? What if high cooking temperatures themselves contribute to the production of the relevant toxins?

Papers in focus

Boschelli, F. (1993) 'Expression of p60$^{v\text{-}src}$ in *Saccharomyces cerevisiae* results in elevation of p34^{CDC28} kinase activity and release of the dependence of DNA replication on mitosis', *Mol. Cell. Biol.* 13: 5112–21.

The cell cycle in eukaryotic cells is regulated . . .. Mutations can . . . abolish the usually strict dependence of DNA replication on mitosis [whereby a round of DNA replication cannot begin until the previous mitosis is complete], and strains [of yeast] with these mutations can pass through START and undergo DNA replication without completing nuclear division during the previous cycle . . .

[In transgenic yeast strains called *ura3::v-SRC* strains, the cell cycle appears to stop in the middle of cell division] . . . cells are large budded. The nucleus is located in or near the bud neck in many cases . . . the dumbbell-shaped cells bud further, such that multiply budded cells are present . . .

The large-budded phenotype of the v-Src-arrested cells suggests that the block in cell division occurs after START and before cell separation. However . . . it is possible that further progression through the cell cycle occurs. In line with this reasoning, when v-Src-arrested cells . . . were analyzed by flow cytometry, the peak of fluorescence in the v-Src-arrested cells occurs at a DNA content greater than the 2N peak [indicating a fully replicated genome] in the control strain . . .. Taken together, the microscopy and flow cytometry data indicate that DNA replication proceeds in the absence of mitosis when v-Src is expressed.

In summary, the transgenic yeast cells were found to have stopped dividing in the middle of the cell cycle. Despite this, the cells contained more DNA than could be accounted for by a fully replicated genome. More DNA was apparently being synthesised even though the cell cycle had been interrupted and the nuclei had not divided.

The elevated DNA content resulting from v-Src expression might be explained by a failure to exit S phase [the part of the cell cycle where DNA is replicated], with multiple rounds of DNA replication ensuing [and no progression at all towards cell division]. This possibility is unlikely [the author goes on to give reasons] . . .. The observations are more readily explained by invoking passage from mitotic entry to S phase without mitotic exit occurring [i.e. a new round of DNA replication starts in the middle of mitosis, rather than waiting for the end of mitosis].

The interpretation was that the chromosomes were undergoing another round of replication even though the previous round of nuclear division had not finished. The author concluded that in the transgenic strain, the checkpoint that prevents DNA from being replicated until after the previous mitosis had failed.

Boschelli, F. (1994) 'Retraction: expression of p60[v-src] in *Saccharomyces cerevisiae* results in elevation of p34[CDC28] kinase activity and release of the dependence of DNA replication on mitosis', *Mol. Cell. Biol.* 14: 6409.

In the original article describing the effects of v-Src expression in *Saccharomyces cerevisiae*, I concluded that v-Src caused loss of cell cycle checkpoint control. This conclusion was based mostly on . . . analysis, in which the DNA content increased beyond the 2N level of cells with a fully replicated genome. In response to other investigators' objections that an increase in mitochondrial DNA content could account for the . . . data, I repeated these experiments [with some additional refinements. The results were those that] would be expected for an increase in mitochondrial DNA.

In this brief article, the author reinterprets his results. The observations were correct: the cells had indeed stopped dividing in the middle of the cell cycle, and their DNA content had indeed gone on increasing. However, the increase now seemed to be due to *mitochondrial* DNA replication and not to another round of *chromosomal* replication. The cell cycle control was intact: the chromosomes were, as normal, prevented from replicating again because the nuclei had not yet divided. The transgenic protein v-Src had simply caused an arrest in the cell cycle, with mitochondrial DNA replication continuing indefinitely.

In this case – as the author is generous enough to acknowledge – it was other researchers in the field who proposed the alternative explanation. When we read papers, we must put ourselves in the same position as those researchers and think outside the box imposed by the author's point of view. It is enormously difficult to do this once we have read the Discussion section and been influenced by what authors say about their own results. That is why I do not hesitate to repeat the advice given in Chapter 4:

☞ Readers should evaluate results before reading the authors' conclusions

It is not usual for the possibility of a misinterpretation to lead to the retraction of a paper. Most commonly, no single experiment can conclusively show which of several possible interpretations is the correct one. In such cases, the truth becomes a matter for debate and consensus is hard to find.

Paper in focus

Carlsen, E., Giwercman, A., Keiding, N. and Skakkebæk, N.E. (1992)
   'Evidence for decreasing quality of semen during past 50 years', *BMJ*
   305: 609–13.

We . . . systematically reviewed the complete international literature
on semen analysis since the 1930s with rigorous selection criteria and
statistical analysis . . .
   The analysis was based on a total of 61 papers published between
1938 and 1990, which included data on 14947 men . . .
   Figure 1 illustrates the relation between mean sperm concentration
and publication year for all 61 publications. Linear regression analysis
of mean sperm concentration weighted by number of subjects in each
publication showed a significant decrease in mean sperm concentration
between 1940 and 1990 from 113×10^6/ml to 66×10^6/ml . . .

**After this statement of the observations (there were further results that are not
quoted here), the Discussion section begins:**

Our statistical analysis based on data derived from the world literature
showed a significant decline in mean sperm count from 113×10^6/ml in
1940 to 66×10^6/ml in 1990 among men without a history of infertility.
However, the crucial question is whether or not the apparent decline is
due to impairment of spermatogenesis. Could it possibly be explained
by methodological variation in evaluating sperm concentration or to
differences in racial, geographical, or other aspects of the populations
studied?

The authors discuss that question at some length, before concluding:

Thus, we believe that the reported decrease in sperm count reflects a
true biological phenomenon.

The discussion of possible misinterpretations is interesting but,
inevitably, not comprehensive. Here are a few points that are either
discounted or not discussed:

• studies from the USA consistently show high sperm counts. By
  coincidence, the early studies are predominantly from the US,
  while the later ones are predominantly from elsewhere. Analysis of
  all non-US studies shows a much more modest decline that is not
  statistically significant;
• measurement techniques could have been different in the very
  early studies. If the small number of studies before 1970 are omitted,
  the remaining studies show a marginal rise in sperm count over
  time;
• the average frequency of ejaculation may have increased during the

study period. Although subjects were sometimes instructed to abstain for at least three days before providing a sample, longer periods of abstinence increase sperm counts significantly (discussed in Swan *et al.*, 1997). An increase in the frequency of sex and/or masturbation over the study period could have led to a decrease in recorded sperm counts, which may go some way towards explaining the results.

Are these points relevant to the analysis? Do they negate the findings? That depends on exactly what the study claims to be analysing. The point is that without evidence to rule out other possibilities, we should not assume that the conclusion drawn by the authors is the only one consistent with the observations.

Of course, it is unfair to suggest that scientists only consider the most obvious explanation for their results. In both the papers above, for example, we have seen that the authors discussed alternative inter-pretations in some detail. However, we, the readers, must ultimately decide what to make of the experimental data. Piecing together the answers to scientific questions involves detective work. Accordingly, reading papers is a little like reading a detective story: we need to follow the same clues, red herrings and deductions as the investigators. When we read critically, we are always alert, always on the look out for hidden clues, never reliant on the infallibility of the author.

☞ Readers retain responsibility for rating results

We can conceptualise what we are looking out for as *assumptions* and *deductions*. Everyone makes assumptions; the problem is that it may not always be clear what an author is assuming. When an assumption is invalid, deductions based on it are invalid too. In the yeast example, the hidden assumption was that extra DNA in the cell signified another round of chromosomal replication – hidden, because the assumption was not stated explicitly. The logical deduction that followed was that a mitotic checkpoint had broken down. In fact, the assumption was wrong: extra DNA could also signify more mitochondria. In the sperm count example, the assumption (explicit this time) was that factors like sample collection techniques and period of abstinence did not have a marked effect on the measurements. It is hard to prove whether or not this assumption is valid.

The examples above show us that what authors miss can be obscure and not obvious. There is no point pretending that a reader can detect every flaw in every paper, any more than can the authors themselves, or the journal's reviewers. On the other hand, an extra brain can help when it comes to working out what the authors have assumed. Scien-tists try hard to be aware of their assumptions, and will sometimes state them explicitly. However, a lot will be unstated for one reason or another. Often, it is because the assumptions are clear to everyone and are not in dispute. Sometimes, it is because authors do not realise what their own hidden assumptions are, or even because they would prefer the reader not to probe too deeply.

How can we become adept at spotting hidden assumptions? Here are a few suggestions.

- Visualise the experiment being done. Ask yourself what was actually seen and what was inferred.
- Think of all the factors that might be influencing the results. Ask yourself whether the authors have discussed all of them. If not, why not?
- Interpret results in relation to the real world. Ask yourself whether the authors' interpretations make biological sense. If not, treat them sceptically, even if you cannot spot any particular flaw in the method.

☞ **Procedures and results should make sense in terms of the underlying biology**

There is no point pretending that every hidden assumption signals a bad paper. It is completely normal for researchers to assume certain things without stating them explicitly. On the other hand, not every assumption is necessarily valid, and it is up to the reader to judge. Therefore, we need to be in the habit of routinely seeking out unstated assumptions, at least so we can reassure ourselves that they are reasonable.

Lines of reasoning

We have looked carefully at the assumptions made in a couple of papers. Now let us subject some logical arguments to the same scrutiny.

Paper in focus

Feldman, K.W., Bethel, R., Shugerman, R.P., Grossman, D.C., Grady, M.S. and Ellenbogen, R.G. (2001) 'The cause of infant and toddler subdural hemorrhage: a prospective study', *Pediatrics* 108: 636–46.

Because of the recognition that children sometimes are abused, multiple studies have demonstrated a strong association of infant and toddler subdural hemorrhages (SDH) with inflicted head injury [subdural haemorrhage is bleeding beneath the dura mater, the outer membrane surrounding the brain] . . .

It is surprising that a number of recent studies continue to minimize the role of abuse in the cause of subdural bleeding in infants. [The authors give references to several papers suggesting that subdural bleeding can be caused by minor falls] . . .

In contrast to these studies, there is an extensive body of literature that documents the usually benign consequences of normal infant and toddler falls . . .

When attempts are made to reconcile the differences between these contradictory studies, it becomes clear that cultural barriers to the diagnosis of abuse, the intensity of the clinical evaluation, and the methods of data analysis are fundamental problems that must be addressed . . .

The purpose of the [present] study was to determine the most common mechanisms associated with SDH among children who are younger than 3 years.

From March 1995 through December 1998, all patients who had SDHs or effusions [release of fluid beneath the dura] and had not reached their third birthday were evaluated at 2 medical centers . . .

Deliberately inflicted injury is, of course, not generally witnessed by a third party, making definite diagnosis very difficult. Yet failure to diagnose abuse can lead to the further abuse and even death of a child. On the other hand, misdiagnosis of abuse can lead to removal of children from their parents and incarceration of innocent people.

With such high stakes, it is not surprising that the field of child protection is controversial and emotionally charged. Some authors think that doctors may be too keen to leap to a diagnosis of abuse, potentially endangering innocent parents and carers. Other authors think that doctors may be excessively unwilling to diagnose abuse, potentially putting children at serious risk. This paper, for example, finds it 'surprising' that some studies 'minimize' the role of abuse in causing SDH, and cites 'cultural barriers to the diagnosis of abuse'. We should expect the interpretation of results, particularly in such fraught fields, to be coloured by the authors' preconceptions.

This study enrolled all patients of a certain age admitted to two major hospitals with SDH. Certain children were then excluded – for example, those known to have a coagulation disorder that could itself lead to abnormal bleeding. This is clearly a good way of obtaining a representative sample of patients.

The authors wished to find out the frequency of abuse and of unintentional injury as causes of subdural haemorrhage. In order to do this, they needed some way of deciding – independently of the subdural haemorrhage itself – which of the babies and toddlers in the study had been injured intentionally and which accidentally. To make this diagnosis, they devised criteria according to which they could classify children as unintentionally injured (with various degrees of certainty); injured by indeterminate mechanisms; or abused (with various degrees of certainty from 'likely' to 'highly likely' to 'definite').

Likely unintentional: Single vintage, isolated acute SDH; major event history (eg, fall down stairs in a walker, fall greater than 6 feet); developmentally appropriate history; history consistent/discrete, timing appropriate; associated injuries consistent with history . . .

Indeterminate: Single vintage, acute SDH; minor event history (eg, fall <6 feet, fall down stairs) . . .

Likely abuse: Single vintage injury; minor (eg, fall from couch) or no event history; symptoms or signs of more global primary brain injury . . .

These excerpted criteria hinge on whether the injuries are consistent with the history given by the carer. For example, if a carer said that the baby had fallen more than six feet, that would be consistent with an accidental cause of SDH. Similarly, if the child's other injuries were those that might be expected from a fall of over six feet, that would substantiate the carer's story. In such a case, accident would be deemed more likely than abuse. On the other hand, if a carer said that the baby had fallen off a couch, or if the baby had generalised brain injury, abuse would be deemed more likely than accident.

The trouble with these criteria is that they rely on a preconception about what kinds of accident can cause what kinds of injury. If SDH with a history of a minor fall signals likely abuse, then the physicians must already have decided that falling from a couch is unlikely to be the real cause of subdural haemorrhage. Similarly, the authors are assuming that falling from a couch is unlikely to cause symptoms or signs of more global primary brain injury. The paper does not list the brain injury signs in question, so it is difficult to evaluate the authors' assumption, but the signs might be expected to include central nervous system depression, altered respiration or seizure.

Can we be confident that minor falls do not cause SDH or signs of global brain injury? Maybe. The problem is that this paper seeks to answer that very question: how likely is SDH to be caused by accidents such as falls?

As we have already said, the authors faced an extremely difficult task in trying to determine the causes of injuries that were not independently witnessed. It may not be possible do this without making any assumptions at all about mechanisms of injury. Nevertheless, in making the assumptions that it does, the paper succumbs to an element of circular reasoning, which inevitably weakens the conclusions. Here are a couple of examples:

The abused children and children whose injuries were indeterminate both were significantly younger than the unintentionally injured victims . . .

A history of a minor fall assisted in assigning a child to the indeterminate or abused categories. It could theoretically be argued that minor falls in young babies, but not older toddlers, may genuinely lead to accidental SDH. If this were true, then hospitals would see more young babies than older children with a history of SDH following a minor fall. These babies would be assigned to the indeterminate or likely abuse categories, even if their injuries were in fact accidental. In principle, this could bias the average age of those categories towards younger children.

The initial symptoms of the 39 abused children included central nervous system irritability or depression ($n = 17$), apnea or altered respiration ($n = 7$), seizures ($n = 7$), vomiting ($n = 2$), and increasing head size ($n = 2$) . . .

Although the injury mechanisms reported for the abused children were dramatically less serious than that for the unintentionally injured children, their head injury severity was similar . . .

Again, there are potential causes of bias here. Signs of global brain injury assisted in the diagnosis of abuse, so it is not surprising that some of the children diagnosed as abused had signs of brain injury. A history of minor injury mechanisms also assisted the diagnosis of abuse, so it is not surprising that the children diagnosed as abused tended to have histories of less serious injury than those diagnosed as accidentally injured.

Interpretation depends equally crucially on the reasoning process as on the assumptions made. Just as we need to seek out hidden assumptions, so we need to follow the logical structure of each argument and reconstruct each deductive step in order to assess how convincing we find it. In some cases, this is simple. In others, we may have to engage in careful critical reasoning.

☞ Logical arguments should be followed painstakingly

What do you think of Gene MacHine's implication that the rise in cancer deaths in Europe from 1985–2000 indicates failure of the European initiative? What demographic factors should he have taken into account?

READING RESEARCH

If you are following the progress of a scientific argument or theory, sooner or later you will have to take an interest in earlier work in the field. Authors, of course, refer to their predecessors' work all the time. This section highlights the possible risk in relying too heavily on second-hand accounts.

Revisiting the paper trail

Papers in focus

Donnelly, C.A., Woodroffe, R., Cox, D.R., Bourne, J., Gettinby, G., Le
Fevre, A.M., McInerney, J.P. and Morrison, W.I. (2003) 'Impact of
localized badger culling on tuberculosis incidence in British cattle',
Nature 426: 834–7.

Pathogens that are transmitted between wildlife, livestock and humans
present major challenges for the protection of human and animal
health, the economic sustainability of agriculture, and the conservation of wildlife. *Mycobacterium bovis*, the aetiological agent of bovine
tuberculosis (TB), is one such pathogen. The incidence of TB in cattle
has increased substantially in parts of Great Britain in the past two
decades, adversely affecting the livelihoods of cattle farmers and potentially increasing the risks of human exposure. The control of bovine
TB in Great Britain is complicated by the involvement of wildlife,
particularly badgers (*Meles meles*), which appear to sustain endemic
infection and can transmit TB to cattle[1]. Between 1975 and 1997
over 20,000 badgers were culled as part of British TB control policy,
generating conflict between conservation and farming interest groups[2].
Here we present results from a large-scale field trial[3-5] that indicate that
localized badger culling not only fails to control but also seems to
increase TB incidence in cattle . . .

The trial commenced in 1998 and has involved three experimental
treatments: (1) localized reactive culling, which seeks to remove badgers
from small areas in response to TB outbreaks in cattle; (2) proactive
culling, which aims to reduce badger densities to low levels across
entire trial areas; and (3) no culling . . .

Our analysis revealed that the reactive treatment has thus far been
associated with a 27% increase in the incidence of cattle herd breakdowns (P = 0.0145; standard 95% confidence interval of 4.8–53%
increase) when compared with no culling areas. ['Herd breakdown'
refers to evidence of TB exposure in at least one member of a herd].
This result was highly consistent, with more breakdowns than
expected in all nine of the reactively culled areas (Fig. 2) . . .

Our findings may . . . influence the interpretation of experiments
carried out in the Republic of Ireland, where badger culling has been
linked with substantial reductions in the incidence of cattle TB[18]. Past[18]
and ongoing[19] studies compare the incidence of cattle TB in 'project'
areas subject to intensive, widespread proactive culling of badgers,
with that in 'reference' areas where badgers are culled only in response
to TB outbreaks in cattle. As our study demonstrates that reactive
culling is associated with an increased incidence of cattle TB relative to
no culling, the Irish studies (which lack no-culling experimental control
areas) may over-estimate the true effectiveness of widespread proactive
culling.

The last paragraph speculates about the reliability of a study from Ireland (reference 18, which is the paper by Eves quoted below). The logic seems sound: the Irish study compares proactive culling with reactive culling, and concludes that TB incidence decreases in proactively culled areas. However, the present study shows that reactive culling increases the incidence of TB. Therefore, it is hard to tell whether the difference between treatments in the Irish study is due to the beneficial effect of proactive culling or the detrimental effect of reactive culling, or to some combination of the two.

Eves, J.A. (1999) 'Impact of badger removal on bovine tuberculosis in east County Offaly', *Irish Vet. J.* 52: 199–203.

During the period of badger removal the results of the TB testing programme in the project and control areas was monitored (Table 5) . . .

In the project zone [subject to proactive culling] the reactor numbers [numbers of cattle testing positive for TB] declined from 326 in 1988 to 30 in 1995, a drop of 91%, while the APT [number of reactor animals per thousand animal tests] declined from 3.91 to 0.46, a drop of 88%.

In the control zone [subject to reactive culling] the reactor numbers declined from 910 in 1988 to 430 in 1995, a drop of 53%; the APT declined from 3.39 to 2.10, a drop of 38% . . .. In the same period, the national APT increased by 19%, from 2.70 to 3.20 . . .

The control zone probably suffered some depletion of badger numbers over the years because of the repeated snaring in the removal zone [which was close to the control zone]. As the removal zone was cleared of badgers it became available to badgers from the control zone. Farmers in the control zone were very aware of the reduction in bovine tuberculosis in the removal zone and this may have prompted some of them to take independent action against the badgers in [the control] zone.

The method used here is not beyond criticism. As the author points out, the control may have been imperfect because there could have been some proactive culling, as well as reactive culling, in the control zone. On the other hand, there is nothing to suggest that reactive culling in this study increases the incidence of TB. The proportion of reactors in the control zone fell markedly, while the incidence in the country as a whole increased significantly.

This observation rather negates the criticism of Donnelly *et al.* The criticism – that Eves may have overestimated the benefit of proactive culling – relies on the finding that reactive culling increases TB incidence. But Eves finds the opposite.

In fact, we can go so far as to reverse the criticism of Donnelly *et al.* and speculate that Eves may have *underestimated* the benefit of proactive culling. Suppose that reactive culling in the control zone did increase the incidence of TB over what would have happened with no culling, as reported by Donnelly *et al.* What then could have caused the observed 38% decrease in APT? If the decrease was entirely due to sporadic proactive culling by farmers acting independently, then that proactive culling must have been enormously effective. Proactive culling seems to cause a 38% decrease in APT, but in fact its effect is far greater than suggested by that figure. After all, judging by what happened in the country as a whole, we would have expected a 19% increase in APT. Add to that the effect of reactive culling, and we would expect an even greater increase. If a few farmers indulging in proactive culling can turn that expected increase into an observed 38% decrease, then proactive culling is having a huge effect!

This line of reasoning provides a theoretical argument that Eves actually underestimated the benefit of proactive culling – exactly the reverse of what Donnelly *et al.* speculate. Actually, my argument, though it cannot be ruled out, is pretty implausible. A simpler statement would be that the findings of Eves and of Donnelly *et al.* with respect to reactive culling contradict each other for unknown reasons; that the true picture is for the moment uncertain; and that further research is needed.

This example demonstrates the importance of following up references and thinking about them ourselves if we wish to be certain what they say. The argument of Donnelly *et al.* is logical as far as it goes, but it does not tell the whole story. The crucial point that is omitted in the second-hand account of Eves' paper is that Eves finds a distinctly beneficial effect of reactive culling, unlike Donnelly *et al.* Whatever the shortcomings of Eves' paper, the particular criticism raised by the first paper does seem rather far-fetched in the absence of more evidence.

To be fair, Donnelly *et al.* raise their criticism in the spirit of speculation. However, as we have seen, their own logic can be turned on its head to suggest (equally speculatively) the opposite conclusion.

Our last example returns to the subject of childhood injury.

Papers in focus

Alexander, R., Sato, Y., Smith, W. and Bennett, T. (1990) 'Incidence of impact trauma with cranial injuries ascribed to shaking', *Am. J. Dis. Child.* 144: 724–6.

Retinal hemorrhages, a common component of shaking injuries, are not easily explained by impact alone. A study of 54 infants involved in automobile accidents did not document any hemorrhagic fundoscopic findings [i.e. findings of bleeding observed by looking into the eyes], despite the fact that 43 suffered skull fracture as a result of direct trauma.[15] As another possible mechanism of injury, cardiopulmonary resuscitation and trauma, unless abusive, have not been found to be related to retinal hemorrhages.[16] The presence of retinal hemorrhage in children with intracranial injuries, therefore, suggests that a shaking component of the injury exists.

Retinal bleeding, commonly taken to suggest that an infant has been abusively shaken, might in principle be caused by other mechanisms. It has been hypothesised that the increased blood pressure in the veins resulting from cardiopulmonary resuscitation, where the chest is compressed, might lead to haemorrhage in the eyes or brain. Another possibility is that external trauma, for example from a fall or a car crash, could cause retinal bleeding. It is important to know whether these mechanisms, as well as shaking, can cause retinal haemorrhage, because this affects the reliability of retinal haemorrhage as a diagnostic feature of abuse.

The authors of the above paper describe their reference 16 as showing that cardiopulmonary resuscitation and non-abusive trauma are not related to retinal haemorrhage. Let us look at that reference.

Kanter, R.K. (1986) 'Retinal hemorrhage after cardiopulmonary resuscitation or child abuse', *J. Pediatr.* 108: 430–2.

Fifty-four pediatric patients were evaluated for retinal hemorrhage after CPR [cardiopulmonary resuscitation] . . .. Nine were victims of trauma, whereas 45 had no evidence of trauma preceding cardio-respiratory arrest. Among the trauma victims, five (56%) had retinal hemorrhages . . .. In four of these five . . . retinal hemorrhage was a sign correctly raising suspicion of child abuse [although the paper gives no criteria for diagnosing abuse, and does not specify whether abuse always involves shaking. The fifth trauma victim with retinal haemorrhage had been hit by a car] . . .. Among the 45 patients in whom cardiorespiratory arrest was not preceded by an identified traumatic event, only one (2%) had a retinal hemorrhage . . .

It cannot be determined whether the effects of CPR contributed to this infant's retinal hemorrhage.

Six patients had retinal haemorrhage, five in the trauma group and one in the non-trauma group. Of these six, two (33%) had not been abused. One of these patients had suffered non-abusive trauma (a car crash). The other had received CPR, and it could not be determined whether the CPR was a cause of the haemorrhage. Thus the paper does not suggest as categorically as implied by Alexander *et al.* that CPR and non-abusive trauma are unrelated to retinal haemorrhage, so that the presence of retinal haemorrhage suggests shaking injury. After all, in at least a third of Kanter's patients with retinal haemorrhage, there was no suggestion of shaking.

This last example raises an interesting logical point. Kanter's paper suggests that CPR alone does not commonly lead to retinal haemorrhage: only one out of 45 children receiving CPR without a prior traumatic event suffered from retinal haemorrhage. But Alexander *et al.* appear to infer that if you observe retinal haemorrhage in a patient, it is unlikely to be due to CPR and must be due to some other mechanism such as shaking. That inference does not logically follow. Kanter looks at patients receiving CPR and asks what proportion of them get retinal haemorrhages. Alexander *et al.* look at patients *who already have a retinal haemorrhage* and asks what proportion of them have that haemorrhage as a result of CPR.

☞ **It is difficult to get a complete, reliable picture at second hand**

When you read a paper, it is obviously not a sensible use of time to follow up every single reference and read it carefully. It all depends on how crucial a given reference is to what you are interested in. If you were reading the paper by Donnelly *et al.* (the first reference on bovine TB) mainly in order to find out how the authors defined 'herd breakdown', then you would probably not bother reading the paper by Eves. On the other hand, if you were particularly interested in proactive culling and its effect on bovine TB incidence, you would not want to rely on a second-hand account.

Only the reader can decide when and how to apply the principles in this book to a given piece of reading. The secret is to read actively, put yourself in the author's shoes, and never lose sight of the underlying biology.

Summary

- Scientific assumptions are not always stated explicitly. Arguments should be probed for hidden assumptions.
- Deductions may follow flawed reasoning. Arguments should be scrutinised for faulty logic.
- The author's interpretation is not always the only possible one.
- If a paper is crucial for your understanding, read it yourself.

EXERCISE

The following extracts are from real papers. For each extract

1 try to identify any assumptions that have been made and comment on their reasonableness, as far as you can tell from the quoted extract;
2 comment on the strengths of the deduction and interpretation;

3 comment on any weaknesses or limitations of the deduction and interpretation, as far as you can tell from the quoted extract;

4 suggest any points that you would expect to see discussed in the rest of the paper.

1. Dietary supplements that contain ephedra alkaloids . . . and guarana-derived caffeine are widely consumed in the United States for purposes of weight reduction and energy enhancement. A number of reports of adverse reactions to dietary supplements that contain ephedra alkaloids, some of which resulted in permanent injury or death, have appeared in the medical literature . . .

We conducted an in-depth review of 140 reports of adverse events involving dietary supplements containing ephedra alkaloids that were submitted to the FDA between June 1, 1997, and March 31, 1999, and applied a standardized rating system for assessing causation . . .. Here, we summarize our findings . . .

In general, we defined an adverse event as definitely related to the use of supplements containing ephedra alkaloids only if the symptoms recurred with the reintroduction of ephedra alkaloids or when the onset of symptoms coincided with the expected peak plasma concentration of the drug and resolved within an interval that was consistent with the expected duration of the effect of ephedrine. An adverse event was defined as probably related to the use of supplements containing ephedra alkaloids when the majority of the evidence supported the existence of a causal link but one or more aspects of the case, such as time since the last dose, were unknown or there was a minor inconsistency in the supporting evidence, such as a low reported dose . . .

Patient 7 was an apparently healthy 38-year-old man who had been taking two capsules of Ripped Fuel (according to the label each capsule contains 10 mg of ephedrine and 100 mg of caffeine) each morning for one year as directed on the product label (Table 4). On June 6, 1996, he took his usual dose along with a cup of coffee and went jogging for 20 minutes. After returning home, he was talking with his family when he suddenly collapsed . . .. He . . . could not be resuscitated. Autopsy showed mild cardiomegaly with four-chamber dilatation and coronary artery disease, with narrowing of 50 to 75 percent in four vessels. The cause of death was acute arrhythmia resulting from atherosclerotic cardiovascular disease. Subsequent toxicology testing showed blood levels of 110 ng of ephedrine per milliliter (the therapeutic range used for bronchodilation is 20 to 80).[9] An addendum to the autopsy report included the comment, 'ephedrine is a stimulant medication, and as such may have contributed to a fatal arrhythmia in the decedent.'

From Haller, C.A. and Benowitz, N.L. (2000) 'Adverse cardiovascular and central nervous system events associated with dietary supplements containing ephedra alkaloids', *New Engl. J. Med.* 343: 1833–8.

2. Aminopeptidases (APs) catalyze the hydrolysis of protein and peptide substrates from the N-terminus and are ubiquitously found in all three domains, the Bacteria, the Archaea, and the Eukarya . . .

S. griseus aminopeptidase [sAP] is an extracellular enzyme with a preference for large hydrophobic amino terminus residues[18,19] . . .. The structure of sAP has recently been resolved by means of X-ray crystallography . . .

[sAP is inhibited by phosphate, but it is not clear where phosphate binds to the enzyme. Phosphate is a non-competitive inhibitor, and kinetic studies suggest that it binds close to, but not in, the substrate binding site.] Phosphate and phosphate moiety have been shown to bind to positively charged residues such as arginine and lysine.[36] Since the crystal structure of sAP illustrates that there is an arginine residue near the active site (Arg202 . . .),[16,17] arginine modification with phenylglyoxal was performed and the modified enzyme was further investigated. Phenylglyoxal reacts with the guanidinium group on arginine . . . thus placing steric hindrance on the side chain of arginine without altering its positive charge . . .. The modification of [derivatives of] sAP with phenylglyoxal results in a significant change in the kinetic parameters K_i, K_m, and k_{cat} for the hydrolysis of [the synthetic substrate] Leu-pNA . . . [K_i increases, meaning that phosphate is a less efficient inhibitor of the enzyme after its arginines have been modified. K_m increases, meaning that the modified enzyme has a lower affinity for its substrate than the unmodified enzyme. k_{cat} decreases, meaning that the modified enzyme works less quickly than the unmodified enzyme.] . . . These significant changes in catalytic paramaters reflect that arginine is involved in the catalytic action of this enzyme.

Modification of sAP with phenylglyoxal is not specific for any of the 8 arginine residues in sAP. However, if an arginine is involved in phosphate binding, incubation of the enzyme with phosphate prior to modification should protect it from the modification to a certain extent. In addition, since the transition-state analogue 1-aminobutylphosphonate is a strong inhibitor of sAP toward peptide hydrolysis,[37] it should protect an Arg from modification to a certain degree if the Arg is involved in binding of the inhibitor . . .. The protection experiments were accomplished by incubating the enzyme in the presence of an inhibitor . . .

The results reveal that the enzyme samples modified in the presence of phosphate or 1-aminobutylphosphonate exhibit significantly higher activity than the samples modified without any inhibitor . . .. The protection against the modification by the transition-state analogue 1-aminobutyl phosphate (which bind[s] to the active site of the enzyme) reflects that the modified arginine(s) must be in very close proximity of the active site, which leaves Arg202 as the most probable candidate . . .. The modification of Arg202 and its involvement in phosphate binding is further corroborated by the observation that the analogous AP [aminopeptidase] from Aeromonas, which does not have an Arg residue close

to the active site . . . is not inhibited by phosphate at basic and neutral pHs and is only very weakly inhibited . . . by phosphate in a competitive manner at pH 6.0.

From Harris, M.N., Bertolucci, C.M. and Ming, L.-J. (2002) 'Paramagnetic cobalt(II) as a probe for kinetic and NMR relaxation studies of phosphate binding and the catalytic mechanism of *Streptomyces* dinuclear aminopeptidase', *Inorg. Chem.* 41: 5582–8.

3. [A]n average of 225000 hair mineral tests . . . are performed yearly by 9 laboratories in the United States . . .

Hypothesising that there should be no significant variations between test results on scalp hair from a single donor, we performed a small evaluation of interlaboratory agreement among laboratories currently offering these tests . . .

Six laboratories were selected, based first on laboratory volume of hair analyses and second on lower sample weight requirements . . .

Hair was donated by 1 author, a generally healthy 40-year-old white woman, with untreated brown hair . . .. Hair cuttings measuring 3.2 cm from the scalp were combined, mixed, weighed, and divided into the amounts required by each laboratory . . .

All laboratories advertised CLIA [Clinical Laboratory Improvement Act] certification in their client brochures. Follow-up with the [regulatory agency] confirmed that laboratory B had misrepresented itself as CLIA-certified [and was therefore operating illegally] . . .

Many reported values [for mineral content of hair samples] showed great differences [among laboratories]. Twelve elements with nonzero reported values have an order of magnitude or greater difference between the highest and lowest value . . .. Outliers were identified in 14 elements' high value(s) as statistically significant ($P < 0.05$) extreme values compared with the same element from other laboratories. Laboratory B reported extreme high values for 13 elements, and laboratories D and E each reported 2 elements with extreme high values . . .

Conflicting interpretation and dietary recommendations were observed between laboratories. For example, laboratory E identified the patient as a 'fast metabolizer' and recommended a dietary increase in purine-containing protein and dairy products and abstention from vitamin A supplementation. Laboratory A identified the patient as a 'slow metabolizer' and [gave the opposite dietary advice] . . .

The primary limitation [of the study] was the amount of uniform scalp hair sample available for analysis. Obtaining scalp hair from 1 donor at 1 point in time was a crucial aspect of the study design. This necessarily limited the selection of laboratories receiving a split of the sample to 6 of the 9 identified US laboratories. It also was not possible to assess intralaboratory variability through the use of duplicate samples sent to each laboratory . . .

We found significant interlaboratory differences in reference ranges, hair test values, and interpretations . . .

Hair analysis of individuals for trace elements and nutritional balance is generally unreliable . . .. Health care choices based on these analyses may be ineffective or even detrimental to the patient's overall health.

From Seidel, S., Kreutzer, R., Smith, D., McNeel, S. and Gilliss, D. (2001) 'Assessment of commercial laboratories performing hair mineral analysis', *JAMA* 285: 67–72.

4. One of the mechanisms that bacteria have developed to survive in unfavorable conditions is the ability to respond to stress situations. This stress response is mediated by a changed pattern of gene expression that typically results in an increased tolerance of the bacteria for the stress factor that triggered the response and usually also for a number of other stress factors . . .

To investigate whether induction of heat shock genes results in increased pressure resistance, wild-type MG1655 [*E. coli*] cells were subjected to heat shock and subsequently were pressurized. Heat-shocked cells were strongly protected against HHP [high hydrostatic pressure] inactivation, showing hundreds-fold higher survival than non-heat-shocked cells upon pressurization at 250 MPa . . .. In addition, the increase in *dnaK* transcription after heat shock treatment paralleled the development of increased HHP resistance . . .. Much lower levels of *dnaK* induction and of HHP resistance occurred when the heat shock treatment was conducted in a buffer in the absence of nutrients (data not shown). Taken together, these results strongly suggest that the protective effect of heat shock on the HHP inactivation of *E. coli* is due to the induction of heat shock proteins . . .

Basal expression levels of *lon*, *clpPX*, and *dnaK* [transcription] during growth at 37°C in LB broth were strongly elevated in pressure-resistant mutants LMM1010 and LMM1030 and were slightly elevated in pressure-resistant mutant LMM1020 compared to the pressure resistance of parental strain MG1655 . . .

From Aertsen, A., Vanoirbeek, K., De Spiegeleer, P., Sermon, J., Hauben, K., Farewell, A., Nyström, T. and Michiels, C.W. (2004) 'Heat shock protein-mediated resistance to high hydrostatic pressure in *Escherichia coli*', *Appl. Environ. Microbiol.* 70: 2660–6.

5. There is now extensive evidence that several pathological functions of the human immunodeficiency virus type 1 (HIV–1) Tat protein are mediated by the interaction of Tat with cellular protein Purα . . .

Tat is an RNA-binding protein that stimulates transcription of HIV-1 through a specific interaction with an element (transactivation region, or TAR) present within the untranslated leader of HIV-1 transcripts . . .

Purα is a highly conserved, eukaryotic sequence-specific single-stranded DNA-binding protein. Purα also binds to RNA, although with much lower affinity . . .. Although the Tat-binding domains of Purα have been mapped . . . the regions of Tat that interact with Purα have not yet been determined . . .

Purα, isolated from either eukaryotic cells or bacterial sources, is complexed with RNA. It has been reported that this RNA presence

is important for binding to DNA . . . and to the HIV-1 Tat protein . . ..
With regard to Tat, this raises the question of whether association with
Purα involves binding of both proteins to a given RNA species or
whether RNA optimizes a direct interaction of Purα with Tat. To address
this question, we have removed the RNA initially complexed with GST-
Purα and replaced it with a single-stranded oligonucleotide to which Tat
does not bind. [GST-Purα is a 'fusion protein' produced in vitro, in
which Purα has been fused with the unrelated protein GST to aid purifi-
cation]. Figure 3 shows that treatment of GST-Purα with RNases A and
T1 significantly restricts the ability of Purα to bind Tat (cf. lanes 2 and 6).
The addition of the single-stranded DNA, purine-rich upTAR element,
an excellent Purα recognition element, partially restores Purα Tat-
binding activity (lanes 3–5) . . .. It has previously been reported that Tat
does not itself bind upTAR [Krachmarov *et al.* 1996]. This result demonstrates that oligonucleotide binding optimizes a direct interaction
between Purα and Tat. The addition of the DNA oligonucleotide to non-
RNase-treated Purα inhibits binding to Tat (lanes 7, 8). Since this DNA
does not interfere with the Purα-Tat interaction (lanes 3–5), it is likely
that it is interfering with RNA binding to Purα. This result would suggest
that RNA is more effective than DNA at optimizing the Purα-Tat interaction. It is clear that Tat and Purα interact directly rather than through
an RNA or DNA intermediate, since upTAR does not bind Tat, and that
either polynucleotide has the capacity to configure Purα to bind Tat.

From Wortman, M.J., Krachmarov, C.P., Kim, J.H., Gordon, R.G., Chepenik, L.G.,
Brady, J.N., Gallia, G.L., Khalili, K. and Johnson, E.M. (2000) 'Interaction of HIV-1
Tat With Purα in nuclei of human glial cells: characterization of RNA-mediated
protein-protein binding', *J. Cell. Biochem.* 77: 65–74.

6. In order to evaluate the safety of the intracytoplasmic sperm injection
   (ICSI) procedure [for assisted conception], a prospective follow-up study
   of 423 children born after ICSI was carried out. The aim of this study
   was to compile data on karyotypes, congenital malformations, growth
   parameters and developmental milestones . . .

   A widely accepted definition of major malformations was used, namely
   malformations that generally cause functional impairment or require sur-
   gical correction. The remaining malformations were considered minor.
   A minor malformation was distinguished from normal variation by the
   fact that it occurs in $\leq 4\%$ of the infants of the same racial group . . .

   Major malformations were found for four singleton children, nine
   twin children and one triplet child. This was 3.3% (14/420) of all babies
   born alive. Defining the malformation rate as (affected livebirths +
   affected fetal deaths + induced abortions for malformations) divided by
   (livebirths + stillbirths) the figures were $(14 + 0 + 2)/(420 + 3) = 3.7\%$ . . .

   Minor malformations were found in 84 children . . . Moreover minor
   anomalies were also found in an additional three children who also had a
   major malformation. Therefore, in all, one or more minor anomalies
   were found in 87 children . . .

The 3.3% major malformation rate in our study is similar to that of most of the national registries and assisted reproduction surveys. We consider here the livebirth malformation rate as this is the one most commonly used, rather than a more precise figure including fetal deaths and interruptions of affected fetuses, as used in only a very few malformation surveys. National registries most often register the anomalies at birth or during the first week of life, whereas in this study follow-up was continued for up to 2 years. Moreover, risk figures in the national statistics are probably underestimated as it is unlikely that the malformation rates are obtained as carefully as in this survey. The reported 14 major malformations in this study, however, were noticed at birth, except for the diaphragmatical hernia that was detected only at the age of 2 weeks (this would reduce our figure to 3.0% in a national register).

From Bonduelle, M., Legein, J., Buysse, A., Van Assche, E., Wisanto, A., Devroey, P., Van Steirteghem, A.C. and Liebaers, I. (1996) 'Prospective follow-up study of 423 children born after intracytoplasmic sperm injection', *Hum. Reprod.* 11: 1558–64.

7. The evolution of antibiotic-resistant bacteria has stimulated the search for novel antimicrobial agents or lead compounds from natural sources. Bacterial populations in seawater and sediments may be as high as 10^6 and 10^9 per milliliter, respectively . . . . As benthic, filter-feeding organisms, mussels are therefore constantly exposed to high concentrations of bacteria of which many may be pathogenic . . . . A variety of antimicrobial factors . . . have been isolated from molluscs . . .

Peptide antibiotics seem to be important defense molecules in all living organisms . . . . Many of these peptides show a high specificity for prokaryotes and a low toxicity for eukaryotic cells, and their mode of action . . . is considered unlikely to lead to development of microbial resistance. These properties have favoured their investigation and exploitation as potential new antibiotics . . .

Fractions [of extracts from mussels] showing antibacterial activity were tested for proteinase K sensitivity . . . . When the antibacterial activity was reduced by more than 50%, the fraction was regarded as proteinase K sensitive.

In the same assay, proteinase K was inactivated by heat treatment (85°C, 15 min). As a control the test fractions were subjected to heat treatment alone. Fractions having reduced activity after both proteinase K and heat treatment were regarded as heat sensitive . . .

Several extracts were toxic to brine shrimp nauplii [newly hatched larvae] . . . . In some cases, toxic activity appears to be high in fractions that also show high antibacterial activity. Whether the same compound(s) is responsible for both activities remains to be clarified. However, some fractions are highly toxic without showing any antibacterial activity . . . and some show antibacterial activity, but little or no toxic activity . . . . From a pharmaceutical point of view it is an advantage when antibacterial drugs have no effect on eukaryotic cells . . .

Since enzymatic digestion reduces the antibacterial activity in some fractions, the active molecules are most likely of a proteinaceous nature. When the proteinase K treatment was performed, the heat treatment was included in the test to ensure that the antibacterial activity detected was not caused by proteinase K itself. The heat labile fractions might therefore also be sensitive to proteinase K treatment and contain proteins and peptides with antibacterial activity.

From Haug, T., Stensvåg, K., Olsen, Ø.M., Sandsdalen, E. and Styrvold, O.B. (2004) 'Antibacterial activities in various tissues of the horse mussel, *Modiolus modiolus*', *J. Invertebr. Pathol.* 85: 112–19.

8. The Erbb2 receptor tyrosine kinase is a member of the epidermal growth factor receptor (Egfr) family . . .

Upon receptor activation, specific tyrosine residues in the terminal tail of the receptor are autophosphorylated . . . and then serve as potential binding sites for intracellular signaling proteins . . .

To assess the relative contribution of the different Erbb2 tyrosine autophosphorylation sites, we employed a targeted knock-in strategy involving replacement of the first coding exon of the mouse *Erbb2* gene . . . with the rat *Erbb2* cDNA . . . . Thus, expression of mouse *Erbb2* is disrupted and replaced by expression of the rat *Erbb2* cDNA under the control of the endogenous promoter . . .

Surprisingly, the levels of Erbb2 expressed in the [homozygous knock-in] embryos were dramatically reduced relative to the expression of endogenous Erbb2 in wild-type littermates . . . . However, in spite of the considerably reduced levels of Erbb2 protein, homozygous . . . knock-in animals did not display any obvious phenotype and appeared generally healthy . . .

Consequently, we investigated the effects of further reducing the expression of Erbb2 by interbreeding heterozygous knock-in ($Erbb2^{wt/Erbb2}$) animals [having one copy of the wild-type gene and one copy of the introduced rat cDNA] with heterozygous knock-out ($Erbb2^{wt/ko}$) animals [having only a single copy of the wild-type gene]. This strategy allowed us to express a single *Erbb2* knock-in allele in an *Erbb2*-deficient background to generate hemizygous $Erbb2^{Erbb2/ko}$ animals. Significantly, no [such] animals were found at . . . three weeks old . . .

[W]e assessed whether we could detect viable hemizygous $Erbb2^{Erbb2/ko}$ animals at birth. Although the expected number of animals were present at birth, 18 of the 38 newborn pups were either stillborn or started dying immediately after birth . . . all the dead pups were genotyped to be $Erbb2^{Erbb2/ko}$ animals . . . . These observations suggest that a critical minimum threshold level of Erbb2 protein is required to maintain viability.

Previous in vitro analysis of the tyrosine phosphorylation mutants identified tyrosine 1028 as a negative regulator of Erbb2 [activity] . . .. Accordingly, we next asked whether we could genetically rescue the perinatal lethality observed with the hemizygous $Erbb2^{Erbb2/ko}$ animals, by removing the putative negative regulatory tyrosine residue in Erbb2. This was accomplished by similarly crossing the heterozygous $Erbb2^{wt/Y1028F}$ knock-in animals [having having one copy of the wild-type gene and one copy a mutated rat cDNA with tyrosine 1028 replaced by a different residue] with $Erbb2^{wt/ko}$ animals to generate mice express-ing [a single mutated knock-in cDNA] in an Erbb2-deficient back-ground. Interestingly, in contrast to the hemizygous $Erbb2^{Erbb2/ko}$ pups, no perinatal lethality was observed with the hemizygous $Erbb2^{Y1028F/ko}$ animals.

From Chan, R., Hardy, W.R., Dankort, D., Laing, M.A. and Muller, W.J. (2004) 'Modula-tion of Erbb2 signaling during development: a threshold level of Erbb2 signaling is required for development', *Development* 131: 5551–60.

9. Orally administered retinoids, in particular vitamin A acid, have been found effective [for treating several dermatoses], but serious side-effects . . . have limited the therapeutic use of this drug. In 1975, Ott and Bollag reported very good results with the new aromatic retinoid . . . Tigason . . .

The usual dosage used for the initial treatment with the aromatic retinoid is 1 mg/kg body weight. After 4–8 weeks the dose is often decreased . . .. In a pilot study we . . . found that although the clinical results were good, the side-effects were often unacceptable for the patients . . .. A second pilot study suggested that an additive treatment with topically applied corticosteroids permits lowering of the oral dose of the retinoid . . .

Patients [with psoriasis vulgaris] were randomly assigned to one of the three following treatment regimens:

(1) Aromatic retinoid and placebo cream . . .
(2) Aromatic retinoid and 0.1% triamcinolone acetonide and 5% sali-cylic acid [cream] . . .
(3) Placebo capsules and 0.1% triamcinolone acetonide and 5% sali-cylic acid [cream] . . .

Because it was considered unethical to assign patients to a [placebo capsules + placebo cream] treatment, this treatment was omitted . . .

[The dosage of aromatic retinoid was] about half the dosage currently recommended . . .

[Lesions were given 'intensity scores' at the start of treatment and again after six weeks. Improvement was evaluated by both physicians and patients. The overall improvements were as follows:

	% improvement (physician)	p value vs. active/active treatment	% improvement (patient)	p value vs. active/active treatment
Active capsules/ active cream	55.4		47.9	
Placebo capsules/ active cream	40.8	0.22	38.0	0.38
Active capsules/ placebo cream	18.0	0.0011	8.8	0.0015

Intensity scores were also evaluated separately for two signs (desquamation and erythema) on six body areas] . . .

The [active/active] treatment was . . . more effective than the active cream alone . . . for all body areas and [almost] all symptoms, although with statistical significance for [only four of the twelve measures] . . .

This first double-blind trial has shown that, in the dosage used, retinoid alone has no effect at all. The combined treatment gave better results than the triamcinolone/salicylic acid treatment alone . . .

In sum, we can say that the combination of low-dose aromatic retinoid orally with 0.1% triamcinolone acetonide acid and 5% salicylic acid in a cream is . . . at least as effective as retinoid monotherapy in the usual dosage of 1 mg/kg body weight and [gives] markedly fewer side-effects.

From van der Rhee, H.J., Tijssen, J.G.P., Herrmann, W.A., Waterman, A.H. and Polano, M.K. (1980) 'Combined treatment of psoriasis with a new aromatic retinoid (Tigason) in low dosage orally and triamcinolone acetonide cream topically: a double-blind trial', *Brit. J. Dermatol.* 102: 203–12.

10. Since 1963 a programme has been in operation at Monks Wood Research Station to examine the mortality causes and the pollutant contents of various predatory birds found dead in Britain. Our aim in this paper is to report some of the findings of this study for the 35-year period 1963–97, notably on trends in the numbers of sparrowhawks *Accipiter nisus* and kestrels *Falco tinnunculus* received, and on the seasonal patterns and causes of their deaths . . .

The carcasses we used came from most parts of Britain in response to advertisements placed frequently in bird-watching magazines and journals. We requested all carcasses of certain species, regardless of location and cause of death . . .

The following categories of death were distinguished:

(1) Accident/trauma victims . . .

(2) Shot birds . . .

(3) Starved birds . . .

(4) Diseased or parasitized birds . . .

(5) Poison victims . . .

(6) Unknown causes were attributed to birds in good condition that could not be allocated to the categories above, and showed no obvious cause of death . . .

Overall, the two species showed marked differences in the frequencies of different mortality causes recorded . . .. In the sparrowhawk, most of the recorded deaths were due to collisions or other trauma (65% of all records), while starvation was the main natural cause of death (18% of all records). In the kestrel, only 35% of recorded deaths were attributed to collisions or other trauma, and another 40% to starvation . . .

The relative importance of different causes of death changed over the 35 years of study.

From Newton, I., Wyllie, I. and Dale, L. (1999) 'Trends in the numbers and mortality patterns of sparrowhawks (*Accipiter nisus*) and kestrels (*Falco tinnunculus*) in Britain, as revealed by carcass analyses', *J. Zool. Lond.* 248: 139–47.

11. MDMA ("ecstasy") has become a popular recreational drug internationally . . . In the 1980s, [users generally took] no more than one or two 75- to 150-mg doses, about 1.6 to 2.4 mg per kilogram of body weight (mg/kg), twice monthly . . .. More recently . . . partygoers regard the drug as safe and consume multiple doses during the night . . .

Experimental animals treated with MDMA show evidence of brain serotonin neurotoxicity . . ., and MDMA-induced serotonin neurotoxicity may also occur in humans . . .. Virtually all animal species tested until now show long-term effects on brain serotonin neurons but no lasting effects on either brain dopamine or norepinephrine (NE) neurons . . .

We used nonhuman primates to evaluate the neurotoxic potential of a dose regimen modeled closely after one often used by MDMA users at all-night dance parties. Squirrel monkeys . . . were given MDMA at a dosage of 2 mg/kg, three times, at 3-hour intervals . . .. Of five monkeys treated with MDMA, three tolerated drug treatment without any apparent difficulty. One monkey became less mobile and had an unstable, tentative gait after the second dose, and therefore it was not given the third planned dose. The fifth monkey . . . died within hours of receiving the last dose of MDMA. Two weeks after MDMA treatment, the three monkeys that tolerated drug treatment were examined for chemical and anatomic markers of brain serotonin neurons . . ., along with three saline-treated control animals. These studies revealed lasting reductions in [both chemical and anatomical markers of brain serotonin neurons].

These same monkeys had marked reductions in various markers of striatal dopaminergic axons . . .. The profound loss of striatal dopaminergic axonal markers was consistently observed in all monkeys examined . . .. The loss of dopaminergic axonal markers was greater than the loss of serotonergic axonal markers . . .

To determine whether the severe long-lasting decrements in dopaminergic axonal markers in squirrel monkeys were unique to this primate species, we tested the effects of the same MDMA regimen in baboons . . .. Again, one of five animals died . . .. A second baboon appeared unstable after the second dose of MDMA and therefore received only two of the three planned doses . . .

Neurochemical and quantitative autoradiography studies again revealed a profound loss of striatal dopaminergic axonal markers . . .

The present findings challenge the commonly held notion that MDMA is a selective brain serotonin neurotoxin and carry important public health and scientific implications.

From Ricaurte, G.A., Yuan, J., Hatzidimitriou, G., Cord, B.J. and McCann, U.D. (2002) 'Severe dopaminergic neurotoxicity in primates after a common recreational dose regimen of MDMA ("Ecstasy")', *Science* 297: 2260–3.

    N.B. This paper has been retracted by the authors. See Ricaurte, G.A. *et al.* (2003) *Science* 301: 1479.

12. The arbuscular microrrhiza (AM) is a mutualistic interaction between fungal species from the order Glomales (Zygomycetes) and roots of most terrestrial plants . . .. The key feature of this symbiosis is the arbuscule, a highly branched haustorium-like fungal structure within root cortical cells, that constitutes the symbiotic interface of nutrient exchange . . .

The biosynthesis of carotenoids in response to colonization by AM fungi is indicated by the accumulation of various carotenoid degradation products (apocarotenoids) in AM roots [including mycorradicin, a component of the yellow pigment of maize and wheat] . . .

There are several lines of evidence indicating that the accumulation of the yellow pigment takes place during the disintegration of the arbuscules. Kinetic experiments showed that accumulation of the yellow droplets as well as increased amounts of extractable mycorradicin were not observed at the early stages of the root mycorrhization. Roots with first mycorrhizal structures did not contain either increased amounts of mycorradicin or any significant formation of yellow droplets. One week later, yellow colored mycorrhizal root segments could already be seen with the naked eye . . . mycorradicin was responsible for the yellow coloration . . .. The time period between the first observation of arbuscules and the beginning accumulation of mycorradicin corresponded roughly with the life span reported for arbuscules . . .. Electron microscopy did not allow a definitive localization of the yellow pigment, but provided additional evidence for a connection of the degradation of arbuscules and accumulation of the yellow pigment. We observed large numbers of hydrophobic droplets specifically in mycorrhizal root sections and particularly abundant close to disintegrating arbuscular structures.

Taken together, our results indicate that the apocarotenoids constitut-
ing the yellow pigment are produced during the degradation of
arbuscules . . .

From Fester, T., Hause, B., Schmidt, D., Halfmann, K., Schmidt, J., Wray, V., Hause,
    G. and Strack, D. (2002) 'Occurrence and localization of apocarotenoids in arbuscu-
    lar mycorrhizal plant roots', *Plant Cell Phyiol.* 43: 256–65.

13. The present series of studies [investigates] the influence of using a for-
    mal assessment instrument on preschool teachers' beliefs concerning
    which skills and abilities are important for young children to master . . .

    It was hypothesized that using an assessment instrument causes
    teachers to view the skills and abilities assessed by the instrument as
    more important for children to attain than they would otherwise. If this
    is indeed the case, then teachers who have been using the [formal
    assessment tool called] MAPS should rate a selected sample of its items
    as more important for children to learn than teachers who do not use
    the instrument.

    [We presented a sample of 514] teachers with a number of items that
    described developmental skills and abilities that young children might
    demonstrate. Teachers were asked to rate how important they thought
    each of these skills and abilities were for preschool-age children to learn
    . . . (1 = not at all important, 2 = somewhat important, 3 = important, 4
    = very important, and 5 = critically important) . . .

    As predicted, MAPS users rated the MAPS Language and Literacy
    items significantly higher than non-users (Ms = 3.0 and 2.74, respect-
    ively), $t(512) = 3.78$, $d = .36$, $p < .001$. They also rated the MAPS Early
    Math items significantly higher than non-users (Ms = 3.14 and 2.85,
    respectively), $t(512) = 4.76$, $d = .46$, $p < .001$.

    Importantly, the tendency for the MAPS users to evaluate items more
    favorably than non-users was restricted to the skills and abilities
    assessed by the MAPS and did not represent some general tendency on
    the part of this group to be more positive in their evaluations [as shown
    by a further experiment].

    The above results demonstrate that teachers who used the MAPS
    believed the skills and abilities assessed by it were more important for
    children to learn during the preschool years than teachers who were not
    using the instrument. This pattern of findings is consistent with our
    hypothesis that using the instrument causes teachers to view the items
    assessed by it as more important for children to learn than they would
    have if they had not used it.

From Kowalski, K., Douglas Brown, R. and Pretti-Frontczak, K. (2005) 'The effects of
    using formal assessment on preschool teachers' beliefs about the importance of vari-
    ous developmental skills and abilities', *Contemp. Educ. Psychol.* 30: 23–42.

14. Invasive aspergillosis [infection with a fungus of the genus *Aspergillus*] is
    a major infectious complication in patients with prolonged neutropenia
    and in transplant patients . . .

    Voriconazole is a new broad-spectrum triazole that is active in vitro against various yeasts and molds, including aspergillus species . . .. We undertook an open, randomized trial comparing the efficacy, safety, and tolerability of voriconazole with those of amphotericin B [the standard therapy] for the primary therapy of immunocompromised patients . . .

Patients received primary therapy with either voriconazole [at a specified dosage] or intravenous amphotericin B deoxycholate [at a specified dosage]. Patients with an intolerance or no response to the initial therapy could be switched to other licensed antifungal therapy and continue to be included in the analyses. The planned duration of therapy was 12 weeks. Administration of study drugs was discontinued in cases of severe adverse events [or certain specified changes in blood biochemistry] . . .

The median duration of voriconazole treatment was 77 days . . .. Other licensed antifungal therapy was given to 52 patients [out of 144] in the voriconazole group. The first other licensed antifungal therapy was amphotericin B deoxycholate in 20 patients, a lipid formulation of amphotericin B in 14, itraconazole in 17, and a combination in 1.

The median duration of amphotericin B treatment was 10 days . . .. Other licensed antifungal therapy was given to 107 patients [out of 133] in the amphotericin B group. The first other licensed antifungal therapy was a lipid formulation of amphotericin B in 47 patients, itraconazole in 38, and another antifungal drug or a combination of drugs in 22.

The outcome at week 12 . . . was significantly better in patients receiving voriconazole . . .

This open study compared two management strategies for invasive aspergillosis, one of which reflects the common clinical practice of treating patients with conventional amphotericin B and then changing drugs as dictated by the occurrence of toxic effects or a lack of response. Patients treated according to this strategy fared worse in terms of efficacy, toxic effects, and survival than those who instead began treatment with voriconazole.

From Herbrecht, R., Denning, D.W., Patterson, T.F., Bennett, J.E., Greene, R.E., Oestmann, J.-W., Kern, W.V., Marr, K.A., Ribaud, P., Lortholary, O., Sylvester, R., Rubin, R.H., Wingard, J.R., Stark, P., Durand, C., Caillot, D., Thiel, E., Chandrasekar, P.H., Hodges, M.R., Schlamm, H.T., Troke, P.F. and de Pauw, B. (2002) 'Voriconazole versus amphotericin B for primary therapy of invasive aspergillosis', *New Engl. J. Med.* 347: 408–15.

15. Fungi and bacteria constitute the main components of the soil microbial biomass. It has often been stated that fungi are more tolerant of heavy metals as a group than bacteria . . .

In the present study, the effects of Cu and Zn on bacterial and fungal activity, as well as on total microbial activity (respiration), were compared in a laboratory experiment using artificially contaminated soil. First, the short-term effect was monitored for a week. Our hypothesis was that fungal activity would be less negatively affected by heavy metals than bacterial activity, while total activity would be between these two measurements. Second, the long-term effect of metal additions was monitored over a 60-day period. The objective was to compare the rates of recovery of the different activities over time . . .

Bacterial activity, measured as the thymidine incorporation rate, decreased linearly with the logarithm of the metal addition above a metal concentration of $2\,mmol\ kg^{-1}$ (Fig. 1B). No differences were observed between effects due to Zn and Cu contamination. The highest levels of metals decreased bacterial activity to less than 10% of that in the control samples . . .

Fungal activity, measured as acetate-in-ergosterol incorporation, increased with the added soil metal concentration above $4\,mmol\ kg^{-1}$ (Fig. 1C). The increase was most evident for the Cu-contaminated soil, where the highest level of Cu addition increased fungal activity seven times. In the Zn-contaminated soil, fungal activity in the soil with the highest level of contamination was three times higher than that in the control samples . . .

The fungal activity actually increased with metal load within a few days after metal addition (Fig. 3C), which was unexpected. This increase was most evident in the Cu-contaminated soils, which also had the largest increase in relative fungal/bacterial ratio (Fig. 6). One explanation may be that fungal growth, like that of other soil microorganisms, is carbon limited . . .. The extra carbon released from dead bacteria would thus trigger increased fungal growth, overriding the negative impact of the heavy metals. Bacteria, which were negatively affected by the metals (Fig. 1B), apparently could not take advantage of this extra carbon. The observation may also, of course, partly be due to problems with the techniques.

From Rajapaksha, R.M.C.P., Tobor-Kapłon, M.A. and Bååth, E. (2004) 'Metal toxicity affects fungal and bacterial activities in soil differently', *Appl. Environ. Microbiol.* 70: 2966–73.

16. We have . . . been trying to identify all the DNA polymerases in [a] hyperthermophilic archaeon, *Pyrococcus furiosus*, that . . . grows optimally at 100°C . . .

[We cloned *Pyrococcus furiosus* genes into *E. coli* and prepared cell extracts. We then heat-treated the extracts and looked for residual heat-stable DNA polymerase activity] . . .

[A region containing two *P. furiosus* ORFs (open reading frames, i.e. polypeptide-coding stretches of DNA) called ORF2 and ORF3 was inserted into an expression vector]. The heat-treated cell extract from *E. coli* . . . transformed with the resultant expression plasmid . . ., in which the genes for the two ORFs were arranged in tandem, exhibited a strong DNA polymerase activity. In order to determine which gene is required for DNA polymerase activity, the two ORFs were independently inserted into [the expression] vector and each was expressed individually in *E. coli* host cells. Sonicated and heat-denatured crude extracts from strains producing either one of the two ORF proteins did not carry DNA polymerase activity. However, when the two extracts were mixed together, the activity was revived. The recombinant proteins were purified to near-homogeneity by sequential column chromatographies of extracts from *E. coli* strains expressing the ORF2 or ORF3, or strains which co-produced both ORFs . . . .. DNA polymerizing activity could only be detected in the presence of the two proteins, regardless of whether they were purified individually or together . . . .. On gel filtration columns, the DNA polymerase activity was eluted at a retention time that corresponded to a molecular mass of 218 kDa, which is in accordance with the sum of the molecular weights of the deduced amino acid sequences of the two ORFs (data not shown). From this, we deduced that the active complex is a heterodimer made up of a 1:1 ratio of the two proteins.

From Uemori, T., Sato, Y., Kato, I., Doi, H. and Ishino, Y. (1997) 'A novel DNA polymerase in the hyperthermophilic archaeon, *Pyrococcus furiosus*: gene cloning, expression, and characterization', *Genes Cells* 2: 499–512.

REFERENCE

Swan, S.H., Elkin, E.P. and Fenster, L. (1997) 'Have sperm densities declined? A reanalysis of global trend data', *Environ. Health Perspect.* 105: 1228–32.

Appendix

REFERENCES FOR THE EXERCISE IN CHAPTER 4

1. Sumpter, D.J.T. and Beekman, M. (2003) 'From nonlinearity to optimality: pheromone trail foraging by ants', *Anim. Behav.* 66: 273–80.
2. Walters, K.-A., Tipples, G.A., Allen, M.I., Condreay, L.D., Addison, W.R. and Tyrrell, L. (2003) 'Generation of stable cell lines expressing lamivudine-resistant hepatitis B virus for antiviral-compound screening', *Antimicrob. Agents Chemother.* 47: 1936–42.
3. Nishimoto, S., Kawane, K., Watanabe-Fukunaga, R., Fukuyama, H., Ohsawa, Y., Uchiyama, Y., Hashida, N., Ohguro, N., Tano, Y., Morimoto, T., Fukuda, Y. and Nagata, S. (2003) 'Nuclear cataract caused by a lack of DNA degradation in the mouse eye lens', *Nature* 424: 1071–4.
4. Georget, M., Mateo, P., Vandecasteele, G., Lipskaia, L., Defer, N., Hanoune, J., Hoerter, J., Lugnier, C. and Fischmeister, R. (2003) 'Cyclic AMP compartmentation due to increased cAMP-phosphodiesterase activity in transgenic mice with a cardiac-directed expression of the human adenylyl cyclase type 8 (AC8)', *FASEB J.* 17: 1380–91.
5. Togna, G.I., Togna, A.R., Franconi, M., Marra, C. and Guiso, M. (2003) 'Olive oil isochromans inhibit human platelet reactivity', *J. Nutr.* 133: 2532–6.
6. Banci, L., Bertini, I., Cramaro, F., Del Conte, R. and Viezzoli, M.S. (2003) 'Solution structure of Apo Cu,Zn superoxide dismutase: role of metal ions in protein folding', *Biochemistry-US* 42: 9543–53.

Index

Index of Papers in Focus and papers by subject